FOOD REPUBLIC

Editors: Ann Ang, Daryl Lim Wei Jie, Tse Hao Guang

Cover: Lim An-ling (musingcats.com)

Published by
Landmark Books Pte Ltd
5001 Beach Road
#02-73/74
Singapore 199588

Landmark Books is an imprint of
Landmark Books Pte Ltd

ISBN 978-981-14-5856-9

Printed by Oxford Graphic Printers Pte Ltd, Singapore

FOOD REPUBLIC

A Singapore Literary Banquet

Editors

Ann Ang
Daryl Lim Wei Jie
Tse Hao Guang

LANDMARK BOOKS

TABLE OF CONTENTS

INTRODUCTION

I

Brilliat-Savarin, the French epicure and pioneer of food writing, once famously said "Tell me what you eat, and I will tell you what you are." I know he said that not because I'd read anything he'd written, but because it was the quote that opened each episode of the cult '90s Japanese cooking show Iron Chef. Iron Chef was crucial in my gastronomic formation and rumination.

For readers not familiar with it: the series featured Chairman Kaga, a gastronome who founded a "Kitchen Stadium", a cooking arena for challengers to contest his Iron Chefs: allegedly invincible experts in various cuisines. It had over-the-top theatrics (episodes had a theme ingredient, which Kaga would unveil by pulling away a cloth, allowing the ingredient to dramatically rise onto the stage, with equally dramatic music and the use of dry ice). It had flamboyant clothing (Kaga had a full leonine Koizumi-style head of hair, and was dressed much like Brillat-Savarin himself, in the style of the eighteenth-century European aristocrat); it had feuds and memorable battles (who can forget the Ohta faction, who challenged Iron Chef Japanese Masaharu Morimoto at every turn because they hated his fusionist, experimental take on Japanese cuisine?). And it had pathos and emotion (like when Chen Kenichi, Iron Chef Chinese and son of Chen Kenmin, Japan's "Father of Sichuan Cooking", was challenged by his late father's top apprentice, Takashi Saito, who had been tasked by the elder Chen to "Please look after my son Kenichi").

What Iron Chef led me to realise, at the tender age of seven or so, probably while snacking on a pack of Hello Panda and pairing each panda with a squiggle of tomato-flavoured Twisties, was that food could matter a lot to people. They would spend a lot of money on it (the grocery bill alone for the show ran up to US$7 million, or approximately S$12 million in those days). They would fight and defend it. And it was a matter of honour, integrity, heritage, history and identity.

Food was never simply sustenance.

II

As Singapore's food culture evolves, grows and in some ways sadly atrophies, we have developed a heightened sense of appreciation, connoisseurship, loss and even crisis, a mélange of sentiments that has led to interesting cultural, political and psychical developments – changes in the Singaporean psyche.

The Government has submitted a formal bid to inscribe Singapore's hawker culture on the UNESCO list of the "Intangible Cultural Heritage of Humanity". Food-related nostalgia has surged, allowing companies to commercialise and commodify this emotion for sale, whether in the form of tutu kueh-shaped earrings, or iced gem-shaped soft toys, or chicken rice-flavoured chips. Worry about the succession planning of famed hawkers has grown – and interest in supporting young hawkers too.

This is sometimes presented as a stage of siege: the lack of manpower, high costs, a low birth rate, an elite that will pay $15 for ramen but not $5 for char kway teow, a tide of globalisation that threatens to scour us clean, with identikit restaurants serving the same dreary brunch food drenched in truffle oil and mentaiko. And the list of closed heritage restaurants and hawkers lengthens, a psychic Cenotaph of our glorious dead: Glory Catering, Chin Mee Chin, Singapura Restaurant... But these are the only the ones that made it to the papers. Who can ever know our privately lamented losses? And who will lament our private impending losses?

Where I grew up, in Sims Drive, there was an incredible lor mee stall that sold a version of lor mee that offered the option of mee pok, which accompanied the crispy freshly fried fish impeccably. I've not been able to find lor mee pok since. Please, please let me know if you ever encounter it. I beg of you. (I'm not even going to go into food that has become simply impossible or difficult to find, but here's a quick list since I've gotten into this mood: roti jala, appam, putu mayam, satay beehoon, loh mei/loh kai yik...)

It's definitely not all dirges and requiems though. Our migrant food culture has been revitalised by newer migrants over the years, enlarging our hearts and our stomachs. Mala xiangguo is now ubiquitous. We've gained a much finer appreciation of the cuisine of other parts of China, away from the ancestral South (for many of us, at least).

I've eaten pork sisig and pancit palabok that's entered my dreams.

Jollibee has badly stung the Colonel. When I crave pho, I know there's a little Vietnam in Joo Chiat that will tide me till my next trip there. And even my grandparents, who suffered the depravations and depredations of the Japanese occupation, deeply appreciate a bowl of robust, fragrant ramen. Even as we count our losses, an appreciation of heritage should not result in the fossilisation and museumification of our hawker culture.

It was never static; it was never one culture; it is unique because it is always changing. Even the food we offer our dead has changed with our tastes (this may be ah gong's and ah ma's first taste of salted egg chicken, and damn is it good...). Without innovation and invention, we would never have gotten dishes such as chilli crab, fish head curry, laksa, hokkien mee and bak chor mee. (Not to mention salted egg croissants – actually salted egg everything – prata eggs benedict and erm, cendol xiao long bao. But not Singapore noodles. Those are definitely not Singaporean.)

III

It was my personal obsession with food, and my realisation that perhaps the best way to explore this moment in Singapore's food history was not through straightforward journalism nor research (though those have their place, of course), but through literature, that led to this volume that you're holding in your hands right now. If indeed our current national condition was in some ways a psychic affliction, then the diagnosing and treatment had to be less direct, and more artful. In the words of Emily Dickinson, perhaps what we needed was to tell all the truth about Singapore's food, but tell it slant. Astonishingly, I realised that there hadn't been such an anthology of literary food writing from Singapore. I quickly convened a meeting of makan kakis, and we got to work. (I really mean makan kakis. Our first editorial meeting was at a café in Holland Village. Our second was at Sakunthala's on Race Course Road. And so on...)

What we were interested in, we decided, was not simply the making and eating of food, but the entire food culture: that is to say, the shopping for it, the commercialisation and sale of it, the effect its consumption and deprivation had on us, the love and hate of it, ambivalence towards it, and everything in between. And true to the spirit of our conception of Singapore and its food culture, we wanted a capacious and accommodating definition of Singapore, which means that we have made no restrictions on nationality or topic, but have merely asked that the either the author or the work have a meaningful connection with Singapore. After receiving and reviewing the submissions from our open call, we felt that there was a need to expand the anthology to include published material, to reflect a long history of engagement with our food culture. This is by no means a historical anthology, however, but a curation according to themes.

We came by these themes through a simple, but important, realisation: that when people write about food, they often aren't just talking about food, but usually about something else.

Food has always been a kind of safe space for Singaporeans. In the largely depoliticised, OB marker-rich world of the Eighties and Nineties, food was something we could all have an opinion about and debate fiercely. (Which Jalan Kayu prata? Which Katong laksa? Which Murtabak? Which Maxwell chicken rice? And what are the Malaysians claiming this time?) Another way of seeing it is perhaps that food was a topic for us to test waters with our acquaintances. Having argued, laughed and cried over food, we could then, tentatively, slowly move to other issues, probe softer places. And if we were too intrusive or offensive, we could still make a tactical retreat into the spice of the rendang or the subtle sweetness of the sugee cake.

Food therefore provided an avenue for many of our authors to explore larger, more meaningful and more fraught topics. The appetite for food, or lack thereof, could parallel or counterpoint other passions and desires. The demands, pains and pleasures of tradition. Food as a means of connection, but also hurt and revenge. Food as a way of destablising our tight grip on the world of objects. Food helping us get a grip. Family, of course. But also failed first dates and marriages. Nostalgia too. But also anxiety about the future. And anxiety about the present.

Food courts are quite deplorable, but we hope we've assembled one that will please you. The stalls and their eager hawkers await. Come. Eat.

Daryl Lim Wei Jie
on behalf of the editors, Ann Ang, Daryl Lim Wei Jie, Tse Hao Guang
Singapore, 2020

Come Daily Chicken Rice

the correctness of flavour

Arthur Yap

waiting for the lime sherbert to arrive
mother turned around to her vacuous child:
boy, you heard what i said earlier?
Nowadays, they emphasise english.

boy rolled his squinty eyes to the ceiling.
waitress returned, flustered, and started
on her own emphases:
lime sherbet today don't have.
mango got. strawberry also don't have.

mother, upset and acutely strident:
today DOESN'T have
today DOES NOT have.

boy, beyond any mitigation of flavour:
mango can, anything can.
any anything also can.

the glass of the shop amber-tinted;
boy, facing a tall window, looked malarial
mango and, it being a sunny day,
didn't help the spectrum of quiet light.
strawberry-faced waitress went on mouthing
and serving. mother glared and glowered
over whatever else needed emphasised.
courtesy – nowadays, they emphasise courtesy.
eat healthy – nowadays, they emphasise it healthy.

so mother continued to be trenchant,
boy's squint refused to concede acceptance –
an impasse in an icecream cafe
in which one would endure no let-up
and the other for which immediate realia
hold no truth.

FOOD PARADISE DOESN'T MEAN BAD FOOD DOESN'T EXIST OKAY

Natalie Wang

So many things I hate but still eat
and eat again. Gagging down
warm bottles of chicken essence,
stinking soups and stews and teas
as a yearlong pre-exam ritual.
The salt of my skin when wiping
my face while queuing. The dish
at the end, always too oily, too dry,
too burnt, which I demolish anyway
because to not finish would mean
sweat spilt was for nothing. I can still
feel the fish sliming its way down
my throat while my father shouted at me
to finish my food. After the maid left,
the only thing I recall about our meals
was our spoons scraping styrofoam,
the rustle of coral pink plastic bags.
How I gorged at boyfriends' family dinners
and lay in bed after, bloated
but not sated. I still remember my mother's
steamed egg, grey and lumpy and cold
on the table. My mother, guilting,
as she pressed a damp note in my hand
every Sunday for beancurd and pancakes
before leaving for work. My father, sleeping
on the couch while my mother cleaned
the flour covered floor. How she laid out
his broken noodles and too-burnt tempura
to cool. How her shoulders shook as she sat
alone in the kitchen,
swallowing every bite.

Microwave Cooking Class

Leong Liew Geok

Give yourself a little bit of time to know your microwave;
Always underestimate – better than overcook;
Don't steam until fresh prawns kena haebee –
Prawns expensive some more; or cook soup
One-and-a half-hours on high: matilah!
No soup left to serve for dinner.
You can bargain with your oven:
You want to use MORE; you want to use LESS,
Press. Your wish. You're master.

See this big potato?
Round like brown tua pau?
I put it on the side of the plate for better cooking.
I place it five minutes on HIGH:
I enter desired cooking time –
Donno how to cook; first time:
I press 1 minute 1 minute 1 minute 1 minute 1 minute;
I press cooking power – HIGH – and START;
Big potato five minutes; small potato, also five.
Do not use anything with metal; will cause sparks.
Oven glassware is the best; you can see through
To your sexy microwavy food.

My potato is ready. Pass it round please...
Next, let's cook an egg.
Poor thing – so many people tonight
And only one egg. Puncture the egg yolk
One or two times with a fork:
Still like full moon, see?
Here's a plate of tofu stuffed with pork;

Only two minutes to cook these;
If you cover your plate, it's cleaner, faster.
I already cook potato, five minutes,
Egg, one minute, fifty seconds, MEDIUM;
Easy isn't it? Like playing masak-masak last time.

How about some rice for dinner?
I got a little claypot here – I put
Same amount of water as for rice-cooker;
I cook rice five minutes on HIGH, five minutes MEDIUM.
You can join sequence because your microwave
Has the programme. Cover not cover
Same same lah. Microwave rice is very puffy,
Like Swee Kee. When done, let it stand first,
Take out and stir, then cover; now ready to serve.
Sure, you can cook porridge, curry, all bubur –
Follow your handbook, just programme
And go kai-kai. Who wants to stay in the kitchen?
Got nothing better to do meh?

Microwave is very good for vegetable:
I got one plastic bag; Ah Peh at the market
Give me. I put broccoli inside; wash only,
No water added. I donno how to cook:
Use SENSOR COOK! tap tap tap tap tap tap
Stop at Vegetable Programme. START.
Okay already, before you can sing karaoke.
Like vegetable, don't put water
When you steam fish; after, fish
Become fish soup. If you microwave
Fish ten minutes, no tail left, you know.
Why? The head is bigger than the tail,
One end cook faster. So how?
Foil will shelter and protect your tail,
It won't cook faster than your thick fish-head.
Use aluminium foil with the *non*-reflecting side
Facing out, above fishtail, like this.

If the shining side is out, your tail
Give free sparkler show.

Potato, egg, tofu, rice, broccoli, fish:
A complete meal, right or not?
All in half-an-hour cooking time –
Fast or not?
A lot of hero here tonight:
Nice or not? *Very* nice.
Go home and try, step by step,
Husband and wife together, or separate.
You are master of the machine;
Microwave make everybody more independent,
Now can cook all things for themselves.
With microwave, you must buy more food
And let Ah Lau ka ki choe.

Crabs to Slow Cooking

Ruth Tang

Everyone in this house is sleeping
or grown. In forty years you have not
done either, only the dishes. Which
themselves, like broiling meat, are never
done, either. Dinner cooked, eaten cooked
and eaten, again. Where the comma falls,
meaningless always. Meaningless,
always. We are running out of milk. We
are always running out of milk. Children
do not even like milk; it's merely
what they were told. The same as
you. What they were told and you,
not: leaving is possible. We don't yet
possess the mettle to say necessary. Casement's
unlocked, your second-best shirt clean
and open. Elsewhere you may find new
errands to love, other mouths. Forty
years sitting with shoelaces
undone. Now they are waking
only to recall their
hungers. Come back. Run.

My Mother's Mini Moat

Jinny Koh

After months of trial and error, my mother finally found a way to vanquish her enemies. They were innumerable, seemingly insurmountable. They invaded her pantry, tiny black dots swirling in concentric circles, sometimes making figure eights in the pastries, chips and sweets she left on the table. Some feasted on cereal – the sugar proving too much for their little feet, they would be discovered stuck on the bits of frosting, struggling to break free.

My mother had tried many ways to obliterate them. She bought poison – brown particles of "food" in thumb-sized parcels – and placed it strategically around the house. The plan wasn't just to kill them but to fool them into bringing the poison back to the colony, eliminating the entire army. It worked for a while but they came back eventually, more ferocious than before. She hung small mesh bags containing wood chips on the kitchen walls because the salesman at the market had claimed that the herbal scent would ward them off. Those didn't work for long, either.

In the end, she fashioned a mini moat on the kitchen table. First, she poured a layer of water on a plate and positioned a small bowl on top of it. Then a platter of food, such as sausage buns or duck rice, would be meticulously balanced on the bowl. A food cover would encase the three-tier structure, sealing the edibles safely. If the pests attempted to reach for the goodies, they would drop into the water trap and drown slowly. My mother was surprisingly successful, save the few rebels that managed to float to the sides of the bowl and climb their way up.

The Battle with the Ants was only a small part of my mother's laborious daily conflicts. She demanded all dishes and cutlery be washed with soap, even if they were already clean, before using them. She was afraid that when left unattended, they might be exposed to traces of cockroach or lizard droppings. If I dropped the food cover, I had to clean it with a wet dish towel because it had made contact with the germs on the floor.

My mother didn't keep leftovers, scared that overnight food might spoil or cause cancer, even if put in the fridge. She often backed up her claims with research she had found in newspapers or online – and more recently, WhatsApp. When I was a kid, she would steam my sandwiches before letting me eat them. Everything had to be brought to the mouth piping hot to ensure that all traces of bacteria had disappeared. The same went for sushi and coleslaw. As long as it was cold, she would reheat it into a soggy mess. Once, she saw a head cheese at the supermarket and thought the gelatinous texture looked interesting. She brought it home, excited for us to try. As usual, she popped it into the steamer and was shocked when the aspic melted into a watery sauce studded with floating pieces of ham.

Growing up, I tried not to let her fears rub off on me. When she wasn't looking, I would drink a glass of water without rinsing the cup first. I devoured sashimi behind her back. It was my small attempt at pulling away from her world of untold dangers. I had seen how my mother lived her life in constant worry. I didn't want to be like her.

To be paranoid, to pre-empt dangers before they can be realised, is my mother 's mode of survival. But she didn't always use to be that way. When she was a student, my mother joined the National Police Cadet Corps. She would recount to me her fierce days crawling under barbed wires during training, marching under the hot sun and going on camping trips with her friends. She and my father would go on fishing dates where they sailed straight into the ocean and returned home hours later laden with swordfish, lobsters and crabs.

Those days are well beyond her. She no longer dabbles with adventure, claiming that being a mother changed her since she constantly worried for my safety. I was never fully convinced by her explanation, even more so after becoming a mother myself. While I, too, worry for my children's safety, the level of fear my mother experienced was simply irrational. It took many years, coupled with an increase in public awareness of mental health, before my mother finally decided to see a psychologist to cope with her anxieties and to unlock the truth behind her paranoia – the origins of which she, too, struggles to understand. While I would not attempt to speculate the reasons behind her fear (for mental health is a vastly complicated subject) I am grateful that she has taken steps to address it. Call it a coincidence, but several months after, my mother was diagnosed with breast cancer. One of her greatest fears had indeed materialised, and help to manage her stress and emotional upheavals could not have come at a better time.

My mother is currently undergoing chemotherapy and I am immensely proud of what she had endured and overcome. I saw how brave she was – not because she had conquered her anxieties (they had, unfortunately, and understandably, increased) – but because amidst her struggles, she persevered with her treatments. To this day, she is still terrified before every single doctor's check-up, afraid of what the doctors may discover. She's terrified of venturing out of her house alone, worried she may experience giddy spells. She also hasn't had a good night's sleep, always nervous that something bad might happen in the middle of the night. Her unrelenting fears had found new ways to manifest themselves in her life, but this time around, my frustrations have given way to empathy.

Nine years ago, my maternal grandmother passed away from breast cancer. Since then, four of my six maternal aunts have contracted breast cancer, two of whom did not survive. Even though most breast cancers are not hereditary, the statistics are grim. I try not to let these numbers get to me, though. Now that I don't live with my mother, I make my own house rules. I don't re-wash dishes or avoid leftovers. I own a microwave even though my mother thinks it emits harmful radiation, and I drink cold milk even though she thinks it is too "cooling" for my body.

But some days, as I tuck into a plate of two-day-old spaghetti, I feel my mother's fears rising up in me. Fork in the air, I hesitate for a moment before I catch myself and brush them away.

The Sneeze

Edwin Thumboo

That hawker there,
Selling *mee* and *kway-teow*
Is prosperous, round,
Quick moving.
With practised grace
He blows his nose,
Tweeks it dexterously, secures complete evacuation,
Then proceeds to comply with the slogans,
The injunctions on the need to

Keep Singapore clean –
Keep Singapore germ-free
Keep Singapore...

By wiping his fingers thoroughly on his apron.
He is not going to dirty the drains,
Clutter the spittoons.
He obeys the law,
Deals with his cold seriously.

If you sneeze after a meal
Of *mee* or *kway-teow*
It is really the steaming-hot soup,
The chillies and pepper that discomfort you.

on offal

Arthur Yap

lau lim pored over a stack of brochures —
sanyo, hitachi, national, westinghouse.
a washing machine, a compact dummy-thing
has replaced the dhobi, spreading out clothes to dry.

this man, as job epithets go,
is in the porcine line – stall 27;
his pig-intestine soup diffuses aroma to all.

a pig is a very compact arrangement
and lends itself to gastronomic deconstruction,
every which part is tedious and messy
but no parts more so than the innards –
slippery, slithery ropes to hang
culinary excellence on.

the scraping of the mucilage takes two people
some hours each early morning, a job
of moan and groan. worst of all,
not showing up is total loss of trade to the man
pursuing the brochures with a vengeance.

bypassing light cotton, delicate fabrics,
and other settings, his two sonys whirl and churn
loud and clear. If you look at the glass windows,
grey snakes glide in quick-heavy motion.
and, from the bowels of these machines
to the boiling cauldron, it is a duplicitous movement.

what a congruence
of processes it all is:
the soup arrives,
for you and for you,
steaming in your face.

A Wet Market in Singapore

Leong Liew Geok

Two old geezers are tailing me,
Pointing to this and that, seeding questions
Into plateaus of watercress and spinach, cabbage,
Kangkong, leeks and tomatoes; seas of fish, prawn
Shell and squid. Wherever I go, they follow,
Fingering leaves of tapioca, tiger lily buds,
Smelling pandan, karapuncha and petai.
How soon after will our pee smell of rotting beans?
Can we try a couple raw? Here and now?
What goes into fishballs? The sea cucumber is a slug?
Ah, garoupa of the rocks, tilapia from the farm:
All fish is poetic! The old bard runs two fingers
Along the sandpaper skin of shark. The younger squints
Through glasses at blue, white and green mottled
Flower crabs; he'd like to take them back to New York.
From stall to stall, they conjure inventories – images
And nuances – coughing into hoary beards that this is all
For real. Ambling through plucked fowl and galleries of meat
For corridors of fruit – to brush past cherries, grapes, strawberries,
For longans, lychees, rambutans, water apple, mangosteens –
All in season – they ask for money to buy some of each.
I see them gloat in the large embrace of multitudes, the market men
And women meandering like rivers dragged by the silt of plastic bags
and motley goods.
They are in their element! I am no keeper of shadows
And grubby greybeards drive me up the wall.

Gentlemen, no one leaves without being treated to the king of fruits –
Let me walk you to the durian stall.

Durians

Toh Hsien Min

During my last reservist stint, in Ama Keng,
that unmistakable waft: like garbage and onions
and liquid petroleum gas all mixed in one. We jerked
our helmeted heads upward, and saw the spiky bombs.
Durians. Two soldiers waded into the lallang and long
spiky-grassed undergrowth, sweeping for fallen fruit.
I remembered what my dad once told me,
that durian trees knew when you were underneath
and would not let their deadly payload drop.
They were smarter than we thought; those things could
kill. For when they had spent the years
building up to seed, they did not want to waste
their chance by murdering their postmen.
It spoke husks about why we were there,
stuck in sweatstink and number four fatigues,
when a drive by Dempsey Road could have reaped
D24 fruit from Selangor. I guess we take
what we can get. All the same, I couldn't help
thinking of the Filipino legend, in which a hermit
made a fruit to help a king win over a princess,
then cursed it when the king neglected to invite him
to the wedding feast; and we've been eating it ever since.

Drinking Wine – Two Poems
(Li Bai)

Wong Phui Nam

i

Adrift all day in the warm elation of wine
I wake to the cold surprise of daylight failing
and find me under a dripping rain of flowers
gathering into a pool of petals in my lap.
Still light with wine, I am drawn to the moon
white in clear water, swimming in another sky.
She makes a vacancy of the hour in these hills.

ii

This wine from Lanling breathes a distilled fire
that sears a slow dying bouquet on the tongue.
It glows in the cup of fine jade you raise to me,
a deep and overflowing living warmth of amber.
If you, my host, can help me lose my self all day
in such lightness of being with this good wine,
I will not care where home is. Home is everywhere.

First Addiction

Shirley Geok-lin Lim

"Addiction is like diction: poetry cannot give it up."

What would you like with dinner? she asked
of me and everyone else entombed in the plastic metal room, offering juices of apple,
orange, grape, the tropical pineapple,
sodas of light and dark and bright hues. On the cardboard
lay a cold hard roll and colder hard
tab of butter; stewed meat brown plated
with matchstick carrots, some kinds of starches.
What would you like to drink?

A bottle
of red, I said, brave at newly turning sixty, all
grown up finally, admitted with gods and goddesses,
adults known for their adulteries,
and other heroines in faraway and fabled cities –
Paris, London, Rome. I'd dropped in on these
and always drank water.

Water. For the poor.
The child. The little girl, unthinking, choosing. No,
having water chosen for her. That small
voice rising in a question. The least of them all
waiting to be first, grimly studying the menu,

scraping the cream cheese off the bagel, the Blue
Cheese Ranch off the quarter tomato, stripping
the list to its leanest, skipping the icing
on the cake.

And now that voice speaking
with the drunks, the addle-pated, addicts
of mental runarounds and slurry poetry,
flying above the earth through literally
blue space into night and strange places, joined
with the vagrant, shaman, homeless: wine.

Hymn to Ninkasi

Toh Hsien Min

Friday evening. Mikkeller. Back in the good days
when it was in a forty-footer at Prinsep Street,
you could bring your own fried chicken or satay,
your moccasins rattled the cut gravel underfoot,
and you hoped the sky would not pull its draught
because the container would never fit everybody.
All it needed was winter offset by patio heaters
for that hot-cold checks-and-balances sensation,
but the streetlight orange was ripe with shadow,
and the sheet gold of the IPAs would be bursting
with hoppy citrus peel and passionfruit flavour.
We were always most honest with each other here,
which had the soft comfort of oft-washed shirts,
so I felt a new prickliness against my skin when
you said you hadn't spoken to your dad in years.
Since you told him Caroline moved in, you added.
I thought of the Chemistry professor I had known
and how he had mellowed following my graduation,
so that all the possible reasons were plausible,
and found least among these that he could easily
have cut the woven fibres loosening between you.

The world's oldest surviving recipe is for beer.
It was carved on two 3,800-year-old clay tablets
transcribing a hymn to Ninkasi, Sumerian goddess
of brewing. It records how to handle the bappir,
how to mix in date honey, how to water the malt,
how to brew sweet wort so that the filtered beer
bubbles like the onrushing Tigris and Euphrates.
It has a good resemblance to modern beer brewing

save for the honey. One does the same few things in roughly the same order to get an end product, but if you brew beer seriously you quickly learn how each small variable, whether the temperature or water softness, can send the beer veering off in one direction or another. Perhaps your father had worn a hair-shirt over this, wondering where he had gone wrong. Or else told you he would not stop you if you did not shove it in his face and kept the edifice of his values easy to maintain, but you always drank deep draughts openly, until you danced the dance of Ninkasi. I took you home so often even Caroline shook her head in dismay. "If she were a dude," she sighed, "I'd scold her for being a dick." So I should not have startled when, three pints later, hanging on to lucidity, you confessed it hadn't been your father's fault because it was you who had said you never wanted to see him again. And the old and new caliphates contesting the plain of the Tigris and Euphrates are each too impassioned to see how their war is only playing pass the parcel with the status quo and, like spent grain, cannot dictate the course of the twin rivers lowering themselves into sea.

Useless

Koh Jee Leong

To see for the first time a thing other
than the mire of food
Lee Tzu Pheng, Anne 'Neanderthal Bone Flute: A Discovery'

When she was sucking the bone clean of marrow
at a feast thrown by him for his now woman,
when his now woman snuggled close up to him,
smacking her lips over the bone he'd picked for her,
when everyone agreed what a great feast it was
and congratulated her for being the birth reason,
when she said, in reply, that just four days ago
they had celebrated their third together year,

the once woman put her bone away. For two months
he lay with this now woman before he left her.
She had no words for this useless discovery.
The whole night the marrow bubbled in her mouth.

Neanderthal Bone Flute: A Discovery

Lee Tzu Pheng, Anne

When did she become aware of hunger
the hunters could not feed? When heed
promptings inchoate as stirrings in air,
changes in light, while all bound her
to her assigned role, undeviating labour?
They must have taken her by surprise –
those unwonted visitations, unwanted wakings
– that time when the animal lay hewn,
open, un-dressed for their feasting
or their store. Then, the gnawing was
more than literal, unignorable. She knew,
fingers and teeth gripping the bloody bone,
picking sinew and soft cord clean, sucking
till the air punctured vertebrae, the great
backbone of the beast exposed her, pointing
to the vibrations rising deep within her.

To see for the first time, a thing other
than the mire of food, to – hold it,
a thought coming clear off the pickings that was
herself surfacing out of blood, burden, deadenings;
an other, a secret voice, reverberating breath
that the animal gave her, that was not its own;
she had to capture it, make it hers.
She knew this was power; this, magic.

Now she has many voices; and not one
needs to speak to be heard. Her silence

dusts off millennial layers to recompose
her story. They must listen to her now, learn
to savour anew the air which moved them,
the land singing, earth's fruit on her tongue.

colouring pages for restless restaurant patrons

Anna Onni

these used to be for children to keep them absorbed
while adults talked shop and holidays over plates stacked
high with typical american fare devilled eggs and guacamole
but now the adults have grown fidgety after the customary
greetings and photographs uploaded to feed distant friends
speckled across the map with a time-stamped sequence to
their likes and comments while their children gaze hungrily
at gleaming skins of chicken and the mountain high pile of fries
with cheese and onion dip with dijon mustard and the steak
still oozing red under crisp skin the serrated edge of the knife
is little defence against blue screens straining to dominate the
conversation which has long since stopped between people
obsessed over the many crayon stained paper placemats
that litter the table and underneath it and remain tacked
on walls red snowmen and green princesses because creativity
means colouring outside the lines of conventionality and adults
no longer perturbed by such colour blindness because the real
entertainment is never at the dinner table but the world beeping
in and sending calling cards to mothers in laws who share
marriage advice and suicide cases or kissing the hands of wives
who post a dozen blessings to the world with playground perfect
poses and the husbands scroll through images of bikini-clad nieces
while sharing houseband stories as the sons and daughters leave
the table to let their parents colour in therapeutic mandalas
with stocks and shares and spiritualism of gold and amber rock
and find inner peace in this world of no peace and quiet because
of the screaming babies and tantrum throwing children

dance of the tea eggs

Joshua Ip

“笨蛋，大笨蛋，你什么都不懂” - 沈佳宜

scene: two people slow-dancing in an edm club
chest-laughing after one slapping the other.
your palm stings but the fingers still fit.

afterwards you wanted to eat tea eggs, non-causally.
this be a third-culture thing. every convenience store
is a time warp, but only some have significant snacks.

taxis shorthand regret for a lazy auteur. still, they
keep the non-committal rain out. cold-shouldering me
in this long take, you forget your tea egg in the back seat.

a stair outside your home, the rain outside.
decentered composition. minimal camera movement.
the tea egg raises a smug hand, says “not present”.

sepia cut – i was once introduced, felt home, this worked,
like a kidney. till the drugs expired, and the body rejects.
can you fill that kidney-shaped space with a tea egg?

no freedom to improvise, with no director.
should simmer this moment, and smile like a rice-cooker,
but your eyes are above the legal limit. i should book you.

you are about to something, but where is the soundtrack?
we will need to drunk-sing about this, in separate boxes.
the mtv cut like a trailer. the tune universally recognizable.

Night

Margaret Leong

Night brings a mushroom encampment of tables
along the five-foot way,
In glassless restaurant windows swing
Unfeathered fowl and glistening ducks
Garrotted on executioning hooks;
The waiters clack on wooden clogs
In ragged undershirts and shorts,
As mangy dogs run in and out of monsoon drains,
Where teeming children totter near,
Indifferent to the hands that tender rice;

Now in the neon lights
Toothless women spread their stands
Of cigarettes and melon seeds;
The wayang's wail comes in
An endless,
Long
Disconsolate voice,
Expressive of some private hell;

Upon his cot the jaga quiets down
His restless son; his wife,
Half-veiled, confers with him in personal
murmurs;

Along the streets,
The moving hawkers sell
Their scarlet lichee clusters tied in red,
Their carts so wide, they seem to push
the night along;

Nearby,
And ranged in stalls,
Above some hissing lamps
The cuttlefish are orange and dried
– Lucite, sheer translucency –
And make an incandescent ring
Around a universal dark,
Which stretches forth –
Illimitably.

soft-boiled

Joshua Ip

i burn the toast while reading old love letters
but the eggs are fine. to be sixteen,
when someone squeezes juice for you, perfects a
runny egg for you, spreads margarine
on toast for your convenience, leaves time
to idly ooze your prose across a page.
my sixteen self sopped up the sweetest lines
and sent back stacks of syrup-sogged précis,
but i'm still reading this over my brunch.

between being and becoming, there's a place
familiar, a pleasure in the mush
between the firm and flowing – in the taste
of love soft-boiled, six minutes, surface-deep
in doneness, raw at heart, and young in heat.

Nur's Secret Sambal

Hunger

Alvin Pang

It strikes at the oddest of times: in bed,
while making love, at the best part
of a major blockbuster you're watching
with the girl you want to impress.
Or it could be her scent that drives
you to such distraction, the gnawing
at gut-level, the body's way of blinking
I-want-I-want in a shower, on the train,
in the clutches of a traffic jam. A word,
the faintest wisp of hope which is another
kind of hunger, the slightest brush
of a molecule is enough to set you off
in search of sustenance, enlightenment,
actualisation, sex. All the big names
we use to speak our need, when blood
merely keening its low key of chemicals
sends us running. Call it the pleasure
principle, the way of all flesh, a seed's
restive groping for sunlight, a city's hunger
to spill. Yours might be fame, comfort,
a cold beer, and mine the same
blind thirst for terminal fullness,
the flowering of fruit after a season
of placid dying. Whatever we do
it's never enough, thank goodness.
I'd still like to breathe, fight
the good fight of every step, simple
marvels. Like the pastries I love:
scrumptious buns shaped like fine breasts
and topped with cherries, relish of each bite

and afterwards running home
past the downpour's ache,
the lovely warmth sinking deliciously
into my soaked and wrinkled digits.
What else to want from life
but space in which such rain can fall,
hollow days to fill and fill
before the last sweet surfeit swallows us?

From A Lover's Soliloquy

Eddie Tay

Naked, you can be tasty as honeydew
or sour, like green lemons stolen
from a garden. I was a cold creature
by your bed, watching as you sleep.

I was by your bed, curled up like a worm,
watching as you sleep. Your smile
gave me an apple sweet
from the first day.

I like you best when you are still,
as though you are dead.

Naked, you can be tasty as honeydew
or poisonous, like a fruit plucked too early.
I know it hard
for you to forgive me, and forget.

I know it is hard. The church is hard
as the pavement, hard like a diamond
that cuts. I am tired of nails
and the shadow of Christ.

I like you best when you are still,
as though you are dead.

first date at jumbo seafood

Joshua Ip

a compromising venue, he surmised,
offering her a wholly shellfish menu,
the none-too-subtle proposition – *here,*
i will peel prawns for you, open oysters,
crack crustaceans, muscle open mussels
to tease out sea-sweet, freshly shell-shucked flesh.
for after all, men take the softest
pleasures in the taking off.

she noted though, his intent to unclothe
and opted for a course of more restraint,
requiring less hands-on, practical –
soft-shelled crab, cereal-crusted butter prawns,
fish, skin-on, fried gingerly in soy.
as women have assessed,
some things work better dressed.

From Pulse

Lydia Kwa

More refreshed after the nap, I walk along Joo Chiat, heading toward East Coast Road. It's just past seven o'clock. The light is fading, street lamps starting to come on. I recognise some remnants of the old neighbourhood. Every sensation seems sharper. I feel attentive and vigilant, aware of traces of the familiar, along with their disappearance.

It takes only ten minutes to reach the *kopi tiam*. Noisy at this corner of Joo Chiat Road and East Coast Road, thronging with traffic and punctuated by loud voices. Probably noisier since it's Friday night.

I choose a table outside the coffee shop. There's an occasional breeze that nonetheless feels unsatisfying. The humid air coats my skin with a layer of unease. Maybe it's this very sensation that's making everything seem more acute.

At the next table are a couple of young Chinese men with their female companions. Cantopop flows out from the radio behind the beverage vendor. Sounds like Jacky Cheung, but it's not a song I know.

I order a Tiger beer. The man at the beverage stall scans the bar code on the can before bringing it over. He has an untidy mass of dyed red-orange hair that spills over his forehead, partially blocking his eyes. Punk rocker look. He's probably close in age to Faridah and me. Guess it's never too late to break out.

My can of beer is half empty when I see Faridah walking toward me, dressed in a beige tunic blouse over a long skirt, almost down to her ankles. Her open-toed sandals are rather showy, the row of decorative stones drawing one's attention to the top of each foot.

"Liver 3," I mumble to myself, thinking of the acupuncture point for treating anxiety. My heart starts to beat faster. Faridah's appearance hasn't changed much from the last time I saw her in 2005. A few wrinkles around the eyes and the rare white hair. Surprisingly, no signs of artificial colouring in her hair. But she looks drawn, grief showing in her eyes and the way she carries her body.

"Hello, Nat." She forces a smile as she stands there awkwardly.

I stand up and move toward her, give her a quick hug. She barely responds, her arms limply touching my back before we pull apart. I catch the sweet, heavy scent of jasmine and sandalwood.

I'm amazed to find that the feeling of attraction still exists.

We order bowls of Katong laksa from a stall at the other end of the coffee shop and sit back down.

"I can see..." I begin, but quickly stop myself. What's the point of saying the obvious? Her grief is frighteningly visible.

Her voice is strained. "It feels strange, meeting under these circumstances."

The two men and their female companions are getting rowdy, the men drinking Guinness and the women picking prawns and squids off steaming plates of Hokkien *mee*, fried noodles that were a favourite meal in childhood. I stare past the revellers at the brisk pedestrian traffic. The rhythms around me are chaotic, full of the unspoken throb of desire and anxiety.

"You won't blame me for being preoccupied with Selim, will you?"

"Of course not. Completely understandable."

"The way I found him..." Her eyes redden instantly, and her lips quiver.

I reach out and place my hand on hers while she cries quietly. After a few moments, she gently takes her hand away and wipes her eyes.

"I'm feeling quite mixed up," she whispers, looking down at the ground below the table. "I wanted you to come, and now that you're here, I just don't know what to say. What I need from you. What you can give me."

"Don't think too much about it right now. Just take it easy on yourself."

"I miss our friendship so terribly. I've never dared to speak to you candidly all these years since..." Her voice trails off as she starts to cry again, using her hankie to wipe the tears. She doesn't seem to care that her mascara is running.

"Faridah, maybe it hurts too much to talk right now. A lot of emotion from meeting again. Especially under these circumstances." I clear my throat and stare at the table surface, wondering about the feelings people have to suppress in order to coast through their daily activities.

We eat in silence, in contrast to the customers at the next table, who are now ordering another round of Guinness. When we've finished eating, I suggest, "Why don't we take a walk?"

She looks up at me, somewhat surprised. "Where?"

"What about the back streets in the Joo Chiat area? You lead the way."

We walk along Joo Chiat, heading back in the direction of Cosmic Pulse. I can still conjure up some of the old sites. A red building where the community centre now stands. It was the library I frequented as a child. The place I first encountered Dr. Seuss and *Green Eggs and Ham*. Farther down, there was a bakery on the other side of the street that produced hot, fragrant buns topped with big chunks of rock sugar. The bakery is still there, although I can't smell the same kind of baking.

I feel rather odd walking next to her. Seems intimate and distant at the same time. I have an urge to take her hand, not so much out of lust but because I yearn to connect with the love that existed between us. It's the friendship I most long for. We walk in silence. I wonder if she's also remembering our days as teenagers.

Durian

Catherine Lim

She remembered the time Uncle sent her upstairs to get something for him — it was his spectacles or bunch of keys, she wasn't sure which. She lingered, not wanting to go, for it was dark at the top of the stairs, and Uncle's room was the one in which the old grandfather had died. She lingered, for the terror was mounting and she hoped, by lingering, she would not have to do the errand.

But Aunt had looked up sharply and said, "Go! Does your uncle have to tell you a hundred times?" And Chuan Chuan, knowing the cause of her distress, yelled with spiteful glee, "Upstairs there's a ghost waiting for you! My Grandfather's ghost is waiting for you!"

His mother said, "Don't talk nonsense," and turning to her again shrieked, "Are you going to obey your uncle or not?"

She walked up the long flight of stairs, slowly, while below Chuan Chuan watched with mirthful malice and Aunt with a severity that dared defiance. She went into the darkened room, grabbed the spectacles or keys from the table and dashed downstairs, and in her haste, she fell and hit her head against the wooden staircase pillar. Aunt scolded her for being clumsy, Chuan Chuan laughed hilariously, and while she stood there, gently touching the growing swelling on her forehead, not daring to cry, Auntie Siew Thong from next door came in, and seeing her in this state, clucked her tongue and took her to have some oil rubbed on the swelling.

The recollection of the incident caused her heart to swell – even now, twenty years later – with anger, but it was nothing compared to the incident of the durians. And that she would never forget.

And she remembered the time when she was in the kitchen, taking the shells off a plate of prawns. It was a cold wet day and she was feeling very tired and sleepy. Mechanically, her fingers plucked off the head of each prawn, then the tail, then the shell around the body. She must have dropped asleep, for when she opened her eyes, she saw the cat jumping off the table, and the plate bereft of half its contents. Chuan Chuan who had seen what had happened brought Aunt into the kitchen. Aunt's thin frame quivered with fury, her pinched face took on an expression of concentrated loathing as her hand shot out to pick up the plate and bring it down resoundingly upon her head. Fortunately it was a tin plate. Her head hurt, and she began to cry, whereupon Aunt pinched her arm, crying out, "What? What? You dare to cry?" She hoped Auntie Siew Thong would come in and comfort her, but the neighbour had gone away for a few days visiting relatives in a nearby town.

But the incident did not hurt so much as did the incident of the durians.

She had looked longingly at the fruits — there were two of them, tied together with gunny string. Uncle had brought them in and put them in a corner of the kitchen. The smell of the fruit filled the house; it invaded her nostrils and made her salivate with desire. She knew she would have no share of the delicious thing. Chuan Chuan, clapping his hands as he watched his father put the fruit in the corner, noticed that she too was looking on. He ran to plant himself in front of the fruit on the floor, arms stretched out, to block them from her view, all the time facing her with a challenging glare. With the persistence of a child who cannot bear to take his eyes off a much longed for object, she continued to look at the durians, whereupon Chuan Chuan ran up and pushed her out of the kitchen.

The family went out in the late morning, Uncle to attend to his coffee shop, and Aunt and Chuan Chuan to the temple near the market. She stole back into the kitchen to have a look at the durians. Through a large slit in one of them, she could see the rich creamy softness of the durian flesh. An overpowering desire to taste this flesh drew her swiftly to the fruit; she squatted down, she pushed her small fingers inside the slit and scooped out a portion of the tasty stuff. A mixture of joy and terror causing her small body to quiver, she brought her fingers into her mouth, and visibly thrilled at the deliciousness of the durian flesh. Every bit on the fingers was licked clean; her tongue moved rapidly over the backs, the sides, and when her fingers were thus cleaned completely, her tongue moved slowly over her lips and beyond the lips to the chin, to rescue any smear of the precious stuff there. When it was all finished, she looked around her – nobody was in sight – her fingers shot into the slit again and brought out more soft golden flesh which she devoured just as greedily. And when she finished that, with an effort of will, she made ready to go, after turning the durian round so that the slit that her fingers had invaded would not be seen.

She was full of nervous expectation and when the family came back, she kept her eyes on the ground and did not dare look at them. When, shortly after, she heard a loud cry from Chuan Chuan, followed by Aunt's shrill "Ah Kum, come here at once!" she knew all was lost for her. She went, very slowly, into the kitchen, her face lowered as she stood before Uncle, Aunt and Chuan Chuan in judgement; her eyes fixed themselves on the floor, while the muscles on her body were tensed for an onslaught of blows.

"Did you eat that durian?" asked Uncle, pointing to the fruit, now split open in half, showing a row of soft seeds two of which had had their flesh scraped off them. They stared at her, in forceful testimony. Ah Kum, awkwardly twisting a corner of her dress, said nothing and merely looked at Uncle sullenly.

"DID YOU?" shouted Uncle angrily and without waiting for an answer, slapped the child who began to cry in her small voice. Aunt and Chuan Chuan watched with tight smiles of vindictive triumph.

"Now get out," he shouted and she left the kitchen slowly, still crying softly, while Aunt and Chuan Chuan turned to look at Uncle, incredulous that so audacious an act had deserved so slight a punishment.

The next day, Aunt called Ah Kum to the kitchen. She was sweating and panting apparently after having just come in from the hot sun. In front of her, on the floor, was a pile of six durians, all prised open with the hands to reveal row upon row of golden flesh.

"They're for you, Ah Kum," said Aunt with menacing deliberation. "Every single one of them. Begin eating now." Chuan Chuan stood nearby, grinning savagely.

The sharpness in Aunt's voice and the wicked gleam in Chuan Chuan's eyes had given the order, under other circumstances a delightful one to be complied with immediately, the touch of condemnation. Ah Kum was forced to squat before the opened durians and when she still hesitated, the tears coming into her eyes, Aunt screamed, "Eat! Eat!"

She ate. She ate slowly, uncertainly. The deliciousness of the fruit, as it was brought into her mouth, and her tongue began to work round it, stripping it of the soft flesh, was such as to make her forget her fear, so that for a while, she was actually experiencing sensations of pleasure. Aunt and Chuan Chuan, vexed that pleasure should be part of the punishment and impatient for it to be over, shouted at her, "Eat! Eat quickly!"

They watched, with predatory intensity. And when after the twelfth seed, Ah Kum's face began to take on the pallor of nausea so that she could not bring the durian seed into her mouth but let it stay suspended in her hand, they knew the awaited moment had arrived.

"Eat! Eat!" yelled Aunt and when Ah Kum struggled and retched, a smile came to her pinched face. And now her blood was up. She advanced upon the girl and pointed to the rest of the durians – four of them – and cried, "Four more! You are to eat every one of them, do you hear? Every seed in every one of them!" And mother and son stood by, watching with the lust of vengeance.

But she could not eat more; she was beginning to feel very sick, and the sight of the durians made her feel worse. She felt she was going to throw up very soon. When Aunt and Chuan Chuan saw that she had paused, they rushed upon her and in their anxiety to punish to the full, almost pushed her face down upon the opened fruit.

"Eat! You will not leave the kitchen till you have eaten all!" repeated Aunt. The girl feebly took another seed and brought it to her mouth; her painful efforts at swallowing the soft flesh which her throat and stomach threatened to reject, were watched with delight by the two. A tremendous retching sound, and then the mess flew from her mouth, splattered the front of her dress and trickled down her legs to the floor. She was crying now, she felt so very sick.

"EAT! EAT!" screamed Aunt, all her faculties now attuned to supreme enjoyment of the climax of the torture. The girl would have had her face thrust into her own vomit if Auntie Siew Thong had not come in then. Pleading for her, the plump, kindly neighbour got the girl up from the floor, took her to the bathroom to be washed and changed into new clothes. Then she sent the girl to sleep. Ah Kum, pale and shaken, unrolled her sleeping mat and still sobbing, curled up to sleep.

She was ill for four days. She never looked at a durian again for the rest of her life.

Now, when the durian season came, and everyone brought home armfuls of the fruit and ate with noisy good humour, she looked away for the sight and the smell of the fruit made her sick. The incident, twenty years ago, came back in every vividness of detail; she saw the vomit on her dress, and she smelt its stench. Ah Kum thought with bitterness, "Now that I can afford to buy all the durians I want — and they're the most expensive fruit — I cannot bear to touch it," and her heart swelled in anger against that vicious relative and her son. She heard of them occasionally, but had never seen them since that day she left the house to become a maidservant in another town. Her mistress was good to her, and had allowed her to take up sewing in her free time. After a while she left to become a seamstress and then had married prosperously, her husband being a hard-working, enterprising man who owned a van in which he drove children to their schools every morning, and a noodles stall near a busy cinema, which he operated at night.

The pleasure of prosperity was increased, for Ah Kum, in the reports of its decline in the lives of Uncle and Aunt. Uncle, she learnt from Auntie Siew Thong now fat and grey, but still jovial and kindly, had fallen into debt, had had his coffee shop seized by creditors, and was now in poor health, being lame in one leg and almost blind. Aunt attended him; she went to several houses to wash the clothes, and returned to cook and care for Uncle in their rented room in a dilapidated house. She was as thin and dry as a stick, said Auntie Siew Thong, and each time she had visitors, she complained bitterly about her son, and cursed him, for he had gone off to work in Brunei and never came back to visit his parents or send them any money.

"Not a cent," she said and she was angry because she had heard that he was getting a very good salary. The money from her washing of clothes being inadequate for food, rent and her husband's medical expenses, Aunt borrowed and begged, a shadow of her once proud self.

"It's really pitiful," said Auntie Siew Thong, "they're suffering very much, your uncle and aunt, and although they weren't kind to you when you were a child, that's past and gone and God has punished them enough. Now," coming slyly to the real purpose of her visit, "since you are in prosperous circumstances, you will not mind giving her a present in cash, say, fifty dollars which is nothing to you — your good husband gives you liberally for the housekeeping — but it will mean a lot to her — perhaps a whole month's food. Now God will surely bless your husband with greater prosperity..."

The request was typical of the big-hearted Auntie Siew Thong who spent her days visiting one household after another, ready to aid those in distress, and it was not in annoyance against her when Ah Kum said, with energy, "Never! I'll never forget the day that she forced me to eat all those durians. I was sick, I vomited, but she forced me on! Till my dying day, I will remember this! And now you come to ask me to give her money."

Auntie Siew Thong laughed a little uncomfortably but continued to coax and wheedle. Ah Kum treated her to a large plate of fried noodles, and they chatted about the old days. Auntie Siew Thong looked around the neat, well-furnished house, with the altar to the God of Prosperity crowded with grateful offerings of fruit, sweetmeats, cups of tea and scented flowers.

"You have been blessed indeed!" said the good-natured woman with a sigh, sipping hot Chinese tea after the noodles. "I can still remember you as a child, thin, hungry, frightened and longing for a taste of durian! Now you can afford all the durians you want!"

Ah Kum said slowly, "So Aunt is continually worrying about money?"

"Oh yes, she's always in need of money, and $50 would be so welcome!" cried Auntie Siew Thong, brightening, for she sensed a softening in Ah Kum and was ready to renew her plea for the wretched woman.

"Go and tell her I'm coming to visit her next week, and you may mention the gift, if you like," said Ah Kum with conscious magnanimity.

"You are very good, and so God will bless you and your husband with greater prosperity," cried Auntie Siew Thong, now all smiles, as she prepared to leave and deliver the good news.

The rented room was worse than Auntie Siew Thong had described. It was a small, dark, dingy room, containing the bed of the invalid, screened off by a faded curtain, a kerosene stove and an assortment of old tables and chairs. It gave off the smell of decay and death; everywhere were piles of old newspapers, rags, torn curtains and stained, dented utensils. There were several calendars hanging on the walls, yellowed with age. Aunt greeted Ah Kum with effusive goodwill; she asked her to sit down, enquired about her husband, apologised for the poor state of the room: she said she was too busy with her washing and care of her husband to have time or energy to keep the room in presentable condition. And as she said all this, her small eyes took in the jade-and-diamond ear-rings, the gold necklace, the sleek handbag. Aunt drew aside the curtain and called her husband's attention to their guest. He was clad only in a pair of cotton shorts and he struggled to rise from his bed to greet the guest, but Ah Kum prevented him, saying in a kind voice, "No need to get up, Uncle, no need at all."

He was a wreck of a man, a mere skeleton, his eyesight almost gone, but he smiled and repeated his wife's enquiries about her husband and apologies for the surroundings.

"Go and get Ah Kum a cup of coffee!" he ordered his wife, and she, with the nervous activity of the humble woman visited by important relatives, immediately went to a corner of the room where stood a table with several flasks, containers and utensils, and began making the coffee.

"Oh, no need to trouble yourself!" said Ah Kum exuding magnanimity, her hands on her sleek handbag. Aunt watched those hands, watched for the fingers to unclasp the handbag and bring out the promised cash gift. When Ah Kum stood up, Aunt thought the moment was come, and her eyes glittered with joyful expectation. But Ah Kum was not going home yet, and her handbag remained closed, hanging from her shoulders by its straps.

"I have a present for you and Uncle," she said, "and I have instructed for it to be brought here, as it was not possible to bring it with me."

The present, when it came, required some effort to be brought into the room and placed in it; there was hardly space for the fifteen large-sized durians, so Ah Kum with the amiability of the generous donor, helped the man who brought them to put them under this table or in that corner.

"They're for you and Uncle to enjoy," cried Ah Kum cheerfully. "It's the durian season now, and it will be a great pity to miss eating the fruit."

The look of bewilderment, then of acute disappointment on Aunt's face she did not miss.

"For you to enjoy; durians are so delicious, but so expensive," continued Ah Kum.

"So many for only two of us!" murmured Aunt with a nervous laugh. She turned to her husband and said, "It's durians; Ah Kum has brought durians for us," and her voice laughed nervously; he made to sit up, as if to catch sight of the fruit.

"Eat!" cried Ah Kum with happy generosity. "Eat your fill!" And the thought of the two dining on durians for the next few days because that would save some money on food brought a smile to her lips.

"Eat!" cried Ah Kum with exquisite triumph, "Eat! Eat!"

From "A Lover's Recourse"

Koh Jee Leong

The wine has turned to water, then to vinegar.
The dumbest guest will know it to be vinegar.

Tell me you have not kissed another man since then.
May your mouth taste on every cock my vinegar.

A stone will eat better if seasoned in a sauce.
You let me dip my hunger in your vinegar.

I will say it plainly. My heart is very sore.
My head is swimming. I will write in vinegar.

I want to savor every dish served in the feast.
Why soak all, like the vulgar, in the vinegar?

A common proof of love, they say, is jealousy.
The Chinese thinks that rice invented vinegar.

Before and after hunger, a husband suffers thirst.
Sponge your mouth, Jee, and offer up some vinegar.

From "A Lover's Recourse"

Koh Jee Leong

I read *fulfillment*, and my mouth is filled with honey.
His cock spooned down my throat enormous gulps of honey.

So many nights surveyed the country from afar.
The settlement mornings deepened from milk to honey.

The man I lived with for a year laughs after he comes.
So much excitement, he thinks, for so little honey.

Every day I drink seven cups of instant coffee.
A cough catches my throat, I drink hot water and honey.

My soul will study hard the satisfaction scriptures.
The beaver will build dams. The bee will make honey.

Give him excess, for nothing quite exceeds like it.
Push past the point of honey, there pours still more honey.

Push past the point of honey, Jee, come on the hive,
the humming work, the stings, the wings, the hunk of honey.

Hawker

Ng Yi-Sheng

Mum used to sell bak chor mee. We helped her sometimes, my sister and I, crushing together the lard and mincemeat, snipping the liver into neat triangles, plunging the noodles into scalding hot water. By the end of the day, we'd be coated in grease and sweat, our hands aching with the weight of other people's meals, our fingertips tattooed with blisters.

I remember one night, when I was maybe eleven or twelve, a customer came and ordered a bowl. It was late, and we'd already started to close shop, but mum had us unpack everything from the fridge and serve him, no questions asked.

She sat with him in silence as he ate.

"This is good," he told her, between slurps. "What's your secret?"

This is what she told him:

"Many years ago, I was a bird. And I was no ordinary bird. I was the Phoenix, empress of all feathered creatures, from the hummingbird to the penguin."

"Ah, you should have seen me then. I wore a cloak of golden feathers, brilliant as the sun, and the down on my breast was as soft as a whisper. I rode the winds and trod the clouds so high I could kiss the face of the moon."

"But one day I was careless. I allowed myself to be felled by the arrow of a human hunter. He rescued my body, hurriedly cleansed my arrow wounds with river water, made love to me on the forest floor."

"The gods decided he must be punished. They bound him to a pillar and commanded the creatures of the air to come to his side. So they came: the eagle, the condor and the vulture; the osprey, the buzzard and the kite. They tore at his flesh, stripping muscle and fat and organs from his bones, and left him to die amidst a cloud of midges and flies."

Here, mum wiped her forehead with a dishcloth, and shot a glance at my sister and I. We pretended to be very interested in cleaning the countertop.

"What the gods did not know was that I had given him a gift. Those who are loved by the Phoenix gain the power of rebirth: the ability to rise from the ashes once they are destroyed. And so, as the morning hours pass, my husband heals. The guts grow back in the vessel of his belly, his skin sews itself up, and presents itself anew."

"So each night, the birds of prey rise once again. The falcon, the owl and the kestrel; the secretary-bird, the hawk and the harrier. They carve him up, ripping away each section of his body as if they were clothes on a lover. Stripping him bare."

The customer sat smiling, his spoon suspended midway between his mouth and the broth. He swallowed, savouring the taste.

"And then?"

"As the day breaks, they come to me. Usually I'm in my kitchen, alone after my children have made their way to school. They rush through my window, settling themselves across the cabinets and stovetops, laying down their offerings of meat and gristle, their shining eyes gazing at their Empress. For they know that if I eat of the flesh of my husband, I shall grow back my old plumage, and rise to be with them, walking the heavens as once I did before."

"I accept their tribute. But I do not swallow it. No, I bundle it into Tupperwares. I seal it into my fridge. Then I come here. I mince my husband, I boil my husband, I serve him to the rabble for three dollars a bowl. This is how I repay his debt. This is how I repay my debt. This is how I choose to live the remainder of my days in the world."

The customer had finished his soup now. He rose, bowed slightly, and left the hawker centre, striding into the night. Mum pocketed the money he'd placed on the table, and took care to wash his bowl and chopsticks herself.

Many years later, after her death from ovarian cancer, I came back to the flat to clear out her junk. I found a faded photograph of her hidden in a shoebox beneath the bed. She was young, dressed in a shimmering gold dress. Beside her was a man who had my nose and my sister's lips.

I called up my sister. "Remember the story mum told?" I asked her. She said no, but said she wanted the picture.

The next morning, I woke to the sound of a thousand wings.

And when I reached the kitchen, every spare surface was covered in meat.

Randy's Rotisserie

Amanda Lee Koe

Dinner's been upset across the kitchen floor; she flipped the casserole and then the roast chicken. Obviously this doesn't even make her feel better, because she's still barking. I'm so hungry I actually make a ludicrous lunge to save the chicken, groaning in spite of myself when it hits the floor. At work they would ask me, what happened to your face, these bruises, and I'd say, football scuffle at the bar, or, jujitsu training, injecting elements of masculinity to salve my pride.

Every time she hits me, I wish I were a woman too, so I could conceivably hit back. As it is she comes towards me now, and I grab her right wrist, but she strikes me with the other.

I don't believe you love me, I say, and walk away. She doesn't follow.

I rev the car up and drive out, an aimless, defeated sort of drive, idle contemplations of car crashes and emergency rooms, idle, because they require the sort of certainty and adrenaline that elude me, on and on and on, till –

Randy's Rotisserie, it says in red curling neon.

These girls are standing outside, in spiffy uniforms – yellow shirts and short white skirts – black girls, white girls, yellow girls, brown girls, but all cast from the same mould with perfect teeth and alluring eyes, hands on their hips like race queens at a car show.

I park and cut the engine.

Walking closer, the spits of the rotisserie, rotating lazily, are empty. Completely overstaffed with no roast chicken – good luck to you. I make to head back to my car, wondering where the nearest fast-food chain is, when one of the girls touches me.

Her arm is hot, with a light glaze. As she presses her fingers down on me, it becomes obvious to me that none of them are girls, and all of them are chickens.

She is an item on the menu, a chicken roasting on the spit, except she doesn't have to be on the spit to be roasted, doesn't have to be poultry-sized and dead to be consumed, doesn't have to have feathers to be a bird.

I look at her hesitantly, and she sees that I've understood. She nods encouragingly, and offers me her hand, which is invitingly warm. We go over to the cashier, an oily man with a cowlick, the heft of his pudgy belly showing under a greasy apron. He wipes his hands on the apron before extending them to me.

"I'm Randy," he says in a smooth baritone, just one note too slick, "This is my Rotisserie."

"Nice place," I say casually, then cocking my head to the left slightly towards the girl, "Pretty birds."

Randy gives me a hard look. Right then a man steps in.

"Say, you got any roast chicken left?"

Randy walks out from behind the counter and claps a hammy hand on the man. "I'm not sure mate," he says evasively, "Why don't you go check the spits?"

"Well I already saw them on my way in, and they're empty. Thought I'd come in to ask."

"Then I guess we don't have any, eh?" Randy says, "Sorry 'bout that mate. Next time."

The fellow walks out and Randy's beady eyes flicker to me. He sees that I am trying to digest the exchange.

"Well," he says, rubbing his hands together lightly, "What seasonings do you favour, sir?"

The "sir" is strangely insincere in its deference, but I smile and say, "What do you have?"

The girl sits me down wordlessly with soft gestures, and brings over a menu hard bound in brocade. As she moves I watch her plump bottom wiggle attractively under the tight white skirt.

The menu reads:

Hickory Southern Belle
African Spice
Chinese Imperial Treasure
Traditional Roast
Siamese Delight (seasonal)

"I've got myself here a Southern Belle, don't I?" I say, glancing appreciatively at the girl, making her feel self-conscious, making her feel good. She demurs and titters.

"Yeah that's right," Randy says, "That float your boat?"

"I think we'll do just fine."

Randy turns behind the counter, buzzes an intercom, says "Hickory in 402," and passes me a set of room keys.

He leads me to the back of the shop, narrow and dark, where there is an old-fashioned gated elevator. A grinning man stands by the buttons, dressed in a yellow shirt and white pants. He looks like a carcass, and smells mildly of food rot. He hits 402 mechanically, manically, and then looks at me as if he wishes I could give him more things to press, the grin never leaving his face.

The elevator takes a disproportionately long period of time to reach the fourth floor. A glimpse of the second floor corridor, with a vague windowpane at the end of the corridor casting stained light on heavy dust, mixed in with the stray feather spiraling slowly downwards. The second level feels still, devoid of life.

Sometimes when she's ranting, when she's coming at me, I apply this stillness onto my being, make myself numb to all the nasty things coming out her mouth, treat it as street vaudeville. Toss her an invisible penny in my mind's eye, make it land in her cleavage, stifle a chuckle.

"Was this ever a motel?" I ask my companions. Neither of them answers me. The Southern Belle chicken looks a tad nervous, whilst the elevator operator grins right on. The smell he is giving off is becoming unbearable, and I breathe through my mouth instead. The chicken hears the raspy sound of my breath, and responds to it as if I were whispering her name privately. She puts her hands into my back pockets, and presses her ample breasts against my back.

As we move to hang in the balance between the third and fourth levels, I feel like I am sandwiched by things infinitely larger. The third floor corridor is pitch dark, and it makes of the elevator a coffin, floating suspended. It is so dark that when I close my eyes, the colour behind my lids appears a lighter, friendlier grey.

The surrounding air feels like the consolidation of the weight of every single in-between I had to deal with, the gravity of each decision made, in the moment before it was made. Inconsequential choices; life-changing ones.

When I met her, it was one of those foolish, lovely things, where I knew I wanted to marry her right off the bat, and I made it crystal-clear, and she was flattered. "You haven't seen my other side," she'd said, and I just smiled broadly. I couldn't stop smiling. I was so sure that anything she could lay on me would be worth its while just from being with her.

I feel myself going – where I am going I am unaware of, but surely if I pass through the gated aluminium and into that corridor of nothingness, there is something of consequence waiting for me, a shape fashioned out of a lifetime of opportunity costs – but it is the warm hand in my back pocket that tethers me.

She feels me going forward, and she grabs my ass tightly, presses her hot breasts hard into my back, as if to remind me of reality with sensation, and I am held back by this hand in my pants, these breasts on my back. And the thought that flashes by is: How rude it is for a man to press his hard-on against the tailbone of a stranger in a night club, or a peak-hour train, but how wonderfully soft these breasts are.

As the thought passes, we come through to the fourth floor. There is good artificial lighting, warm and low, and the window at the end of the corridor is boarded up.

The elevator operator throws open the gates, the same smile intact. He shows us to 402, handing over the keys with a small flourish, then shrinks away.

In the room, a large old bed with white sheets, a large carving knife on the bed. One quality linen napkin, with a handsome napkin ring around it. I sit on the edge of the bed and remove my shoes and socks. The chicken props herself against the fluffy pillows, the very picture of docility. I think of my wife, and tuck the napkin neatly into the neck of my shirt.

I carve her up and eat, bit by bit. She is succulent, delicious. The hickory is well-paired with her. We're just missing a red wine. I carve slowly, and she doesn't flinch ever, just looks at me good-naturedly, cooing softly occasionally. I wonder if this would be a bit of a letdown for some men, if they would ask her to writhe and shriek.

It takes me hours, but I'm a very clean eater, I hate to leave meat on the bones. When she's just a carcass, I kiss her mouth and slide her eyelids downwards. Then I remove the linen napkin from my collar and lay it over as much of her as I can, as a courtesy to the cleaner.

I leave the room, walking towards the elevator. The grinning man looks like he's been waiting for me a long time, and ushers me in. The elevator descends much faster than it ascended.

Back out into the store, walking towards the cashier. Randy is seated with his legs propped up onto the table of a booth seat. He comes towards me, passes me the bill. The figures are befitting of a gourmand experience, and I am happy to pay up, leaving a handsome tip.

I ask what his opening hours are. He laughs and wiggles his eyebrows, as if I've fed him a particularly charming inside joke.

Randy rustles the bills between his fingers, then gives me a sidelong look. "Y'know, it's uncommon for us to have walk-in customers at all," he says, "I like you – you're a sharp chap." He gives me a pat on the back and waddles away.

In the car I belch, and it is redolent of hickory chicken. I turn off the A/C, roll down my windows.

Pulling in to the driveway, she opens the front door, runs to meet me, her eyes swollen, puts her arms around me. "I'm so sorry," she says, looking up into my face, "I need to rein in my temper."

I cradle her, murmuring, "It's okay," and she says, "You smell like chicken."

"I had some," I say, "It made me feel better."

"Is that blood on your shirt?" she says, alarmed.

"No," I say firmly, "That's hickory sauce."

We go in, and the mess is still on the kitchen floor. The cheese-smeared broccoli bits and bread-mix, the smashed porcelain deep-dish, the roast chicken; just like the scene of a crime.

It makes me, at once, lose faith in her apology completely, as well as believe, renewed, in just how much I love her. I reach out for the dustpan, wet a rag, and get down on my knees.

From 8 Ways of Loving a Banana

Alfian Sa'at

It was with an alarming degree
Of embarrassment that Kok Leong
Accepted the bunch of bananas
From his parents during that break when
Parents could visit their bald-shaven
Sons in the army camps of Pulau Tekong.
While his other friends received
Biscuits from St. Michael's, Danish
Butter cookies and chocolate eclairs
He was offered a red plastic bag
Bulging with yellow fruit that
Had once been suspended in a room
Clouded with joss smoke to hasten
Its ripening. At night, Kok Leong
Recalled the way his mother fussed
Over his black fingernails and the
Weight of his father's hand on his shoulder.
And wondered how they could have possibly
Known that he had not been able
To pass motion for the past eight days.

SUGAR/CANE

Jack Xi

You are raw as young anger or cut
grass and sweet as melting ice –
rich like a complex or a loving
spank. A ring of condensation
small and thin by the beach.

Yesterday, starved of sand,
I watched you gush and run
        through a plastic cup.
Repeated through a juicer
strong enough to blunt my thumbs.
Lugged bags of your pith to the car.

I watched you grow as a child
beyond my window, fluttering
pennants and stems a cool swath to get lost in.
When my parents first bruised me for red ink
you shook there, row
        on mournful rustling row.
I never ran through you, I was
too busy in my room for my sisters.

Your roots were strewed out
when I looked away. Later, I walked the path
where they made tired and hungry men
tractor you out and pave the crying
dirt in bootprints and machine-cut grass.

I imagined the first bath that coaxed your insides free.
The first person to lift your soft crystal of light,

that glittering hip yet to bloody the dead.

I now drag your remains to the school lab
in short rustling dunes, pith and flakes
        dried on flat bags for marks.

If only every bit of us blinked with round sugar –
if only no candy was birthed from a bruise –
if only every time I broke only love flowed out.
If only pain knew the limits of a small wet cup,
if only every shearing in your life gave you luck –

if only we could sing of the machines that crushed us
knowing at the end it would all be good.

Brunch at Berseh

Brandon Chew

We're in Jalan Besar, Singapore's historical and nominal Main Street; now a bilious four-lane artery clogged with rusty lorries and crusty people. It, and its environs, used to be a swamp in the 19th Century, filled with all manner of murky creatures, before urban planning brought with it the pox of pavement and tar, roads named after luminaries local and foreign, marshals and Muslims. Petain. Kitchener. Hindoo. Syed Alwi. The incursion is long over, and the local fauna have since adapted; today, they lurk in second-storey whore dens and second-hand electronics stores.

The pong of refuse from a nearby dumpster flowers in the afternoon heat as my grandfather leads the way to the Berseh Food Centre. We're late, he says as he walks, his pants threatening to hike up the meridian between his bellybutton and his nipples. Everything might be sold out by now. Paper circles, punched out of parking coupons, dot the footpaths encircling a grass patch next to the multi-storey carpark we use just off the side street.

Berseh is Bahasa for "clean."

Tagging along with us is one of my grandfather's friends, a frumpish old man named...I didn't quite catch it when he got into the car. His face, though, is instantly recognisable as the very archetype of avuncular familiarity. He's every single skinny old man you meet in Singapore, and he's always in pleated pants. He could be having a smoke in your neighborhood coffeeshop, napping at the back of the bus, buying shirts in the department stores of the most fashionable suburban malls – always in the background, a Tzadik in temperate weather.

We picked him up on our way to what I had assumed was a private lunch between grandfather and grandson; two tigers, my grandfather would call us during one of his jaunty moods, separated by almost exactly 60 years and five zodiac cycles. I was only told en route to take a detour to the man's shaded estate in Paya Lebar, which set us back half an hour. After his mumbled words of greeting, he doesn't speak again the entire afternoon.

We're late, my grandfather says again when we reach the Centre.

The golden rule of grandparents is: don't argue.

One does not simply walk into Berseh Food Centre. Not all stalls are created equal, and one must make an informed choice before undertaking the journey. There may be more than one chicken rice hawker in Berseh, but which one marinates his chickens overnight in a secret wet brine? Which one uses only kampung chickens because of an uncompromising recipe handed down from his father, a descendant from the first governor of Hainan? How can a rational person make an informed decision without advance reconnoitring? "Of course I did my research," enthuses a local food blogger. "I knew immediately which stall to target when I went there."

Each hawker worth his or her salt has a legion of vociferous bannermen – grandfathers, gluttons, and everyone in between. Online and in coffeeshops, they trumpet the values of their lieges, who are assigned honorifics – "shiok!," "orgasmic!," "lagi best!" – like feudal lords of old. The uninitiated are told by the faithful that no one else's version is worth trying, and are promised categorical disappointment should they nevertheless choose to worship false gods. Berseh is more than a hawker centre; it is a temple, Mount Sinai, the Tower of Babel.

We – two tigers and a golden-tongued wiseman – walk up to the second floor and settle into a row of tables facing a single food stall in a shady corner. Light pours from a small gap in the roof, as in a church. A man rushes out to greet my grandfather like an old friend. To the delight of all, everything is not in fact sold out, and our orders are taken punctiliously and acknowledged in fluent Hokkien.

Within two minutes, I am presented with two bowls. The smaller holds a gigantic dollop of yam rice, mushy and sticky and brown; the larger bowl, a chipped porcelain old specimen, contains a disappearing delicacy, a brew of secret stock, wolfberries, ginseng and other Chinese herbs with lurid English names. There are some grayish chunks of meat, pork-like in appearance and seabass-like in texture. Half-submerged, they bobble against translucent nuggets of fat lurking closer to the surface. The smell is salty and bitter, as in a swamp.

山瑞汤。Turtle soup. Exactly what you need on a cold winter's night in Northern China. Except this is Singapore: it's thirty-five degrees out, and the single oscillating fan that periodically directs its blades to our table is laughably inadequate as sweat moustaches condense above our lips.

Nevertheless, it's the sole reason we're here. I know a place for lunch, my grandfather had said in no uncertain terms at dinner last week. Pick me up at noon on Saturday. Don't be late.

Now my grandfather grunts in approval. His friend blinks, laconic as ever. They pick up their spoons, and brunch is underway.

I tuck in with some unease; as with all introductions made, there is the expectation of a verdict, an opinion rendered.

很好, I say, nodding with the right amount of awe and respect. The golden rule of grandparents is: any food they recommend is fucking awesome.

I don't have to lie, at least not this time. The soup is medicinally briny, seasoned only with the eldritch bouquet of dried herbs and oleaginous with turtle juice. The meat itself, delightfully tumid on the chopsticks and tongue, tastes exactly like what it is – a hybrid of seafood and game, an animal that belongs both in water and on land, or neither.

At one-fifteen, a man plonks himself down next to my grandfather. No one tells me his name, but he looks like an Alan. Judging by the unwrinkled contours on his face, Alan is at least twenty years younger; judging by the glances exchanged between him and my grandfather, he is late. Alan doesn't apologize for this, nor for his short-sleeved collared shirt, an orgy of bad prints and drooping shoulders in a shade of yellow best called 'scrambled-egg vomit'. In contrast, his hair is alabaster white, his skin slightly less so. Greeting me like an old companion, he jerks his chin approvingly at our bowls, before yelling in the general direction of the drinks stall more than five meters away.

A frothy, frosty Erdinger is soon forthcoming, as is an unsolicited lecture on beers of the world. Alan's current obsession is with lychee flavoured beer, which is apparently all the rage in Hong Kong. Good for the ladies, he says. Or was that, good with the ladies?

After an hour of silent dining – my grandfather is not the most garrulous of men – I sense the opportunity to make small talk. In atrocious Mandarin, I tell Alan about the pilsners and ales I tried while in America, the Budweisers and small-batch brews I discovered in college. My grandfather grunts derisively. He thinks I'm talking bullshit. He's right. I hate beer.

Without having to ask, Alan gets his turtle soup. But before he tucks in, he produces a hip flask from his pocket, unscrews it, and pours its contents into the bowl. Something caramel, glistening like fine glass in the sunlight, cascades into the terrapin morass, and instantly the air is perfumed with the heady scent of burnt vanilla and alcohol.

"Martell. Good shit!" Alan snorts. He orders the hawker to refill my bowl and spikes it liberally and deviously. It's precisely the kind of situation they warned you about in moral education. The golden rule of staying alive is: don't let leering old men pour the contents of an opaque hip flask into your turtle soup.

Politely, we drink. The brandy, complex, filigree, permeates the soup like liquid velvet, slaking spoon and tongue with the illicit, illogical union of bitter Chinese herbs and, well, alcohol. It kind of works.

As we slurp down our second helping of soup, the three old men indulge in some carnivorous nostalgia, going on about a time – "以前" – when dog and snake and entrails could be bought from makeshift roadside stalls and wolfed down by steaming laborers from Guangdong and grown-up Xiamen boys, their homeland proclivities very much alive. Free from the chaste consternation of food courts, sanitation guidelines, and Westernization, the Singapore of old had raised its skirts to them, revealing all manner of earthly delights. Then, my grandfather may have been less likely to raise an animal as a pet than he was to buy it freshly slaughtered at the wet market. Now, one has to quest for a morsel of the exotic, for the tiniest flash of flesh.

Are any places that still sell these disappearing delicacies? Yes, they say, there are old hawkers here and there who still ply the trade, and who obtain their ingredients through shadowy, unscrupulous means. Just the other day, Alan was having a hearty dish of grass snake...somewhere. Nobody wants to give me details. I'm not ready.

At two-thirty, everyone's ready to go. Alan announces that he'll be driving his two companions to Chinatown, where they'll be talking and shooting the breeze over drinks. Two eighty year-olds sitting in a car with a tipsy old retired man at the wheel does not in any way seem like a good idea, but Alan assures us that he is way below the limit, and besides, "there are no bloody police checks in the afternoon!"

I know I'm not invited. My grandfather grunts at me to go home, as if my curfew is at 2 pm, and shuffles off with his friends to the next adventure.

The Berseh Food Centre was so christened presumably to pay homage to the reclamation done around it, the filling of the marshes and farmland with concrete and ash. Before – 以前 – the area was a dank, fertile sprawl of plantations and other agricultural accoutrements. Look closely, though, and you'll find that not all of the swamp has gone away. Strange animals dawdle in bowls of brackish water, while others hunt and eat in broad daylight. The weird lives on in the minds and mannerism of a dying species.

When my grandfather tells me some months later that the stall has closed permanently, its frail owner unable to convince her son to choose the hawker's life, I know that we won't be going back, at least not for the soup. Berseh is a battleground. Petain and Kitchener look on.

Fasting in Ramadan

Alfian Sa'at

God, what am I
But a pale copy
Of the true ascetics?

A lesson in humility,
Only under such heat, such thirst,
Does the soul realise
The body is just a mirage.

Forgive me, God, for
Crossing the dates on the calendar,
Numbering thirty days of abstinence;
For observing how much
Temptation surrounds me.
The tap's mouth glistens even though
It is only my eye that has polished it.

And it is only my longing
That saturates the colour of apples,
That turns a passing scent into form,
Like breaths sculpted in cold weather.

Feasting before dawn.
Each sunrise I fade,
Reduced to a mouth, source
Of desire, of the original sin.
And at each sundown, a glassful of water
Travels down my gullet
And turns me solid again:

God, when you breathed life
Into the first man, was that
What answered his craving?
Or did he know then, that
As you fed him, you also gave him
Hunger, a crumb of that world
That you will cast him down into?

The Queue

Wong May

Queuing
to pay
the queue
was so long
                    I started
                              to eat
the cherries
till half-way
                    I notice
I'll not have to pay
for what I eat
which has a touch
                              of Heaven
in it!
You pay
You pay
          only for what you cannot eat.

Brinjal

Shirley Geok-lin Lim

Fragrant brinjal, purple hazed or
sheen of amethyst; ovaloid female,
pendulous; as shoe polish slicked;
unevenly round, glowing moon's rump
smelling of colours; in farm's wet
morning – ordure of night soil; impenetrable
skin like first sex; shiny as spit,
as slippery; rubbery feel
jousting the palm: you remind
anything in nature is woman's
and man's (overflowing potency,
sultanate of suggestions by river flats),
tickles fancy, excites memory's
warm ooze – these water-smooth firm-toothed
veggies, names jingling like slave anklets
in rattan baskets heaped, abused
by kitchen women, slapped into newspaper wrappers
in the market this morning, fresh talents!

Aubergines

Toh Hsien Min

The purest expression of your love was in your cooking aubergines.
You called them brinjals, after the Indian fashion, sometimes eggplants.
You hated the bitterness you were more sensitive to than I was,
you thought a violet-black face could only bring gall.
In Sanskrit it was vatin-gana, the plant that cured the wind.
Cooked incorrectly, it could be bitter, odd-textured, herald of wind.
You made sure my aubergines were perfect. You didn't panic
when the spongelike flesh drank hissing sunflower oil.
The Arabs knew it as al-badinjan. In Marrakesh,
I had aubergines roasted over a charcoal fire, lightly salted.
You stuck to fried fish, washing it down with sweet mint tea.
We crossed the Straits of Gibraltar, where the fruit became alberengena
and then aubergine. We once dined at Aubergine, in London,
before Gordon Ramsay moved to the Royal Hospital Road,
where he promptly installed a carpet darker than royal purple.
To the east, badinjan became melongena, melanzana, mela insana.
I was your mad apple. The Portugese called it bringella,
and when they landed in Goa their guns brought a word
puréed through innumerable monsoons in the Andaman Sea to you.
In the West Indies, it became, differently, the brown-jolly.
Once the oil hit a fiercely crackling heat, the aubergine's brave
structure collapsed and much of the oil was re-released.
We lease our spirits from our languages. All these names for the same fruit:
the same bulbous expression of energy, pushed through roots
and leaves and stems to still and concentrate as goodness and evil,
shiny and soft. I call them aubergines. You call them brinjals.

Apples

Tse Hao Guang

The purest expression of your love was in your choosing apples.
You called them Jabuka, as the Serbo-Croats do, sometimes Pumu
(Sicilian). You hated that I thought you were so arrogant,
or yaya after the Singlish, like another fruit. I know you used
Google a lot. In French it is pomme, like when you steam
your hair curly. I think the Japanese know it as Fuji. In Meidi-Ya,
Liang Court, I had Shinshu Apple Kit-Kat, which tasted like hairspray.
You stuck to the normal wasabe flavour, and drank all my tee
(tea) (Afrikaans). When you talked to the Makcik she said Malay
is epal, you bodoh, like that also tak tahu. Did you know
across the causeway there is something called the Water
Apple, or Jambu? I can also Google. We once ate at Hans, near
Plaza Singapura, before it renovated, and the floor was yellow
like the apple you are choosing now. I was your bad apple.
Sometimes you bake me in a pie, sometimes I'm pureed, or sliced,
candied, juiced. Once you tried a new recipe and the apples
had to be fried in truffle oil, then the khusabu (fragrance)
(Hindi) can release. Trust Google to help release my lunch.
All these names for the same fruit: the same thing that supposedly
keeps the doctor away, is bruised by the fearsome aunty when
she chiong past you to get the maembe (mango) (Swahili) on offer,
golden and ripe. I call them apples. You call me malu.

Sleeping with Tomatoes

Wong May

I who won't look at tomatoes
Now can't look past tomatoes.

Tomatoes that taste of nothing much.
Now I say beware of tomatoes,

Those that taste
Of anything
At all.

58 Chinese 'nationals' breathed
Their last with packed tomatoes
In a sealed van from Zeebrugge
                                        to Dover.

You think in the dark the tomatoes
          would administer
Oxygen – nothing much
To ask, in the dark.

58 in a van on a ferry
Travelled for better living conditions

"Dying to come abroad",
     With tomatoes for company –
Brilliant!

       Until the driver, amps up the radio –

Like a closet-smoker
Tunes *out* the air-vent.

It's still 6 hours to Dover.
He needs sit back in the lounge, kill time.

When the sealed van opened
The living piled out
The living were tomatoes,
& the dead too.

700 crates, rank
by serried rank,
befalls
The awful lot of Man.

58 thought they arrived
in the United Kingdom.
They don't travel well,
The Chinese,
Without refrigeration.

They were deported
(The bodies,
With refrigeration)
In a fish van.

To be fair
It isn't so long ago
They were burning people.
Now they deport bodies,
& burn furniture.
It took
Just a few dead Latvians
Behind bed-boards
On another P&O;
In Dover they burnt the Ikea flat-packs
for two days.

Burn furniture by all means!
Spare the van.
The van has a future.

Now your tomatoes may
taste Zambian, Romanian
or of the Kurds
With a hint of coriander

& star-anise
: Chinese, as the case may be,
Grill them

They know where the rest are heading
Or hiding.

Trust them
After this Extra/Extra-ordinary Rendition
Trust them
To give just what you want

You who won't look at tomatoes twice

See how they come, these

Moulded like chairs
Red/'wiped clean' factory plastic,

As near odourless
In closed vans

the long haul, by sea

& land, self replicating

These shall inherit your kitchen,

Grill them as they come
Trust me
They are no different.

Swipe them
For the same difference

& you who couldn't even begin to hear/to see
Stand by tomatoes you couldn't now hide
or abide.

I don't pretend it's either human
&/or common.

Just add flames,
(No added sugar)

These know your coming hither
Even as your going hence.

Trust them
Trust us
in time to taste of nothing again.

Dover, June 17th, 2000

Outpouring

Jollin Tan

There was a word
in biology
classes they used
to describe the
pushing motion
in your
oesophagus
and intestines.
Peristalsis.
But it sounds nothing
like the habit
I keep coming
back to, the one
that is familiar
and asphyxiating
like a snug, old
glove that hasn't
quite been worn in.
It doesn't sound
like when I reach
too far back and
everything comes
up too fast, so
I can see the
clear pieces of
food untouched by
the acid of
my hunger.
Peristalsis
only sounds the

slightest bit like
persist, which is
what this monster
(that hides inside
me) does – and that
really is the
only connection.
It is not the word for then
I want to tell you how the ache
is physical – symptomatic – psychosomatic. It's the word
they use in medical terminology, like
when they say things like
compulsion,
eating disorder,
bulimia nervosa,
and all I think is
get out of me.

The Wafer

Gopal Baratham

Justin didn't understand love. This was especially obvious to him when he began thinking about it. But he was certain that he loved Father Rodrigues. The old man had, often enough, spoken about love and as far as Justin remembered all he knew about it was what the Father had taught him.

From their earliest meetings it had been clear that the priest's methods of teaching precluded argument or discussion. Father Rodrigues knew. And felt it his duty to impart this knowledge to his pupil. Justin had come under the Father's tutelage when he was a very little boy. But even then he remembered that when his talk veered towards inquiry the old man would become indignant, then furious. When this happened he had no compunction about using his hard cane on Justin's extremely tender knuckles. Justin remembered this without bitterness. It certainly did not affect the terrible love he felt for Father Rodrigues. And the old man made no apologies for punishment. To him pain was a necessary part of the process by which knowledge was acquired.

Further, the love about which Father Rodrigues spoke so often to Justin was one which included suffering and pain. To Justin love was something warm and comforting. Pain and suffering could not be part of it. It was all so terribly confusing. On the few occasions when he dared question further the old man told him that love conquered all. This produced even more confusion. Did not conquest mean fighting? Suffering? Death?

"Yes. it does. But love conquers all things." And there the discussion, if one could call it that, ended.

***

As the time for Justin's first communion drew near, Father Rodrigues's instruction acquired a frenzied quality. Justin must know enough to make him fit to receive. The old priest's source of inspiration was neither the Bible nor his knowledge of the world which he experienced intimately through the confessional. Oh no. Justin knew that the old man despised some of the younger priests who tried to find common ground between themselves and would-be communicants. This type of instruction, he explained to Justin, was purely temporal. It would lead, in the long run, to conniving with the devil.

From the debris which filled his room Father Rodrigues produced a tattered book of catechism. It was full of questions and resolute answers. These Justin was forced to memorise. How else, he asked, could Justin act in morally difficult situations? When Justin's memory flagged, the Father's anger and cane appeared. At times, however, the old man relaxed and talked about Jesus. He told Justin that Jesus had so loved mankind that he had been prepared to suffer, to be nailed to a cross and die on it so that His body could be eaten for all time and by all men who wished to be saved.

"But how," asked Justin, "could the body of one man continue to be eaten by millions of people for thousands of years?"

"That, my child, is part of the mystery you must accept."

"But is it right, Father, for me to eat the body of another man?"

"Of course it is. Because Jesus, out of His love, chose to suffer not once but again and again so that everyone might be given the chance to learn of his love and be saved."

"But if the Host is really the body of Jesus, would it not bleed as I ate it?"

"It would, Justin. But only if you deliberately bit it."

"But Father, how can I eat it without biting it?"

"You swallow it as gently as you can, showing Jesus that you accept His love and His sacrifice and will not cause Him more pain than He has already suffered." As he spoke, a gentleness came over Father Rodrigues. He put his arm around Justin and pulled him closer. "Love, my child, is not merely kindness. It is not necessarily even gentleness. It involves believing in goodness. And on Saturday you will swallow this belief with the Sacrament."

Justin was happy. He did suspect that the priest was merely rewarding him for memorising his catechism so well, but this did not reduce the warm and wonderful feeling which welled inside him and which he recognised as love. "In just two days, Justin, you will receive," the priest said in a hushed voice.

What, thought Justin, will I receive? A little wafer. Could they not give us a tiny piece of meat, at least?

"It is faith that makes the wafer flesh, Justin," said Father Rodrigues.

For a moment Justin was alarmed. How had the old man read his thoughts? Were there indeed secret powers about which he was unaware and did the old Father possess these? But his alarm was short-lived. The Father's bony fingers rhythmically squeezing Justin's shoulders told him that he was not the first nor the last child to have thought such thoughts before his first communion. Reassured, Justin asked, "Would I really destroy the possibility of Christ's love if I bit into the wafer?"

"No, my child. You would only show that goodness cannot be destroyed."

"And how would this happen, Father?"

"By finding out that when you choose to damage goodness, the only thing you really damage is yourself."

***

Over the next two days Justin did little except wonder about the wafer. How could something with which he was as familiar as ice-cream cones become the body of Jesus? Who would fill the empty holes with blood? There was no way by which something as commonplace as a wafer could become the body of the God he had been taught to fear and love. It was all too absurd. Father Rodrigues was either lying or had become too old to know what he was talking about. And how could he possibly damage himself if he chewed the wafer? There was only one way of finding out.

***

The morning of his first communion was bright and cheerful. Justin bathed and dressed carefully. He shined his shoes and greased and combed his hair. He even put a little talcum powder on his nose to keep it from shining. His appearance must in no way embarrass Father Rodrigues whom he so loved. But he was determined about one thing. He would test his God to whom he was going to be permanently bonded.

As he knelt at the rail he became uncertain. All eyes appeared to be on him. Would he dare bite into the wafer when it was put against his tongue? If he did, would the blood gush out of his mouth and nose? Or would there be some other terrible sign of God's wrath? He felt a slight tingle as the wafer touched his tongue. This was the moment. He could either swallow or bite.

Even as he thought, the wafer began to crumble into his saliva. Then he decided. He screwed up his eyes tightly; then, opening his mouth slightly, bit as hard as he could. A horrible pain filled his head. Saliva flooded his mouth and mingled with it he recognised the salty metallic taste of blood. He swallowed desperately for he knew that if he didn't it would flow out for all the world to see. And why was swallowing so painful? It was a long while before Justin realised that he had bitten deeply into his tongue.

122 Cendol Xiao Long Bao

Nausea Fruit

Daryl Li

I.

In ayam buah keluak, pieces of chicken are braised in a rich sauce together with large seeds from the kepayang tree called the buah keluak. The buah keluak are black in colour and have a unique flavour, which has been compared to truffles. My sister adores this dish. I first learnt of my sister's love for it when we had a Peranakan meal to celebrate my mother's birthday. She loves most of all picking out the kernel of the seed, which gives a black paste rich in umami that explains the ingredient's potent culinary application.

From this seed also comes the deadly poison of cyanide.

II.

The milder symptoms of cyanide poisoning are the sort that may simply be written off as signs of poor health. Headaches, shortness of breath, dizziness. More serious symptoms range from low blood pressure and seizures to cardiac arrest.

It has been used in mass suicide and in genocide. It was used in extermination camps during the Holocaust and also favoured by Nazi leaders as a suicide agent. Unable to keep our violence to ourselves, cyanide is also used for fishing. Cyanide is used in gold and silver mining. With its remarkably high stability in the form of an iron compound, it is also used as an anticaking agent in salt.

This proximity of food to poison is not unusual. From stone fruits and almonds to feseekh and fugu, we live in the midst of potential poisons.

III.

Ayam buah keluak is said to be a quintessential Peranakan dish, but described in those terms, it seems to lose some of its literalness – it is no longer what it is, as though its meaning has been overtaken by the need to signify for something else, be it a restaurant, a culture, or a geography.

My grandmother has no recollection of her biological parents. Her adoptive father, however, was a Peranakan, and she grew up along several other children in a household that I often imagine must have been quite lively. My grandfather's mother was a Peranakan woman whom I've only seen in occasional photographs, all of which are too old and were taken from too great a distance to give me any clear idea of what she looked like.

There is nothing Peranakan about my family at all, although sometimes I feel as though there should be. It is part of a heritage that cannot be connected to my present time, a hidden past that I cannot lay any claim to. The memories do not belong to me. This history is invisible to others, unreadable in my person. The lineage is a part of me, but it is out of reach. Things are both near and far.

IV.

From the richness of its flavours to its distinctive presence in geographical and cultural contexts, ayam buah keluak (and its pork version, babi buah keluak) is an easy dish to love. Unlike my sister, however, my love of the dish is more complicated, more tentative or apprehensive. The dish is something distinctive of Singapore, even if it is not unique to us. It says something of the place I belong to, and yet, doesn't speak precisely of me. It references an inheritance that remains out of reach. It remains external even when consumed, a disturbing distance immune to measurement.

The term "buah keluak" means "fruit which nauseates". At least, that's what I've read. The scientific name is *Pangium edule*, which highlights its edible nature in the word "*edule*", a useful indication for future generations, yet without the warning of possible death.

V.

Cyanide is an oft-used poison in the fiction of Agatha Christie, although she also employed a variety of other poisons as fictional devices. I first encountered her work at a small bookstore in Beauty World that rented books out, which my parents would take me and my sister to every two weeks or so. I think I picked them up on a whim, and quickly fell in love with the stories of Hercule Poirot.

Among the stories featuring cyanide are *And Then There Were None*, *A Pocketful of Rye*, and of course, *Sparkling Cyanide*. There was always something fantastical about it to me, as though the texture of fiction had created a separation between me and the chemical reality of the poison. Cyanide seemed so far away that I would never ever come into contact with it. I had no idea then that it had always been right by my side.

Proximity and distance: a persistent and irregular blur of contraction and dilation, or perhaps a superposition of meanings, a paradox, a potent confusion.

VI.

The tour ends in summer rain. It's always summer rain here. I am walking down the path with two or three others when the director of the Botanic Gardens turns around to explain that that there is a kepayang tree. He introduces us to the tree, saying nothing about it except for the fact that the seeds of its fruit contain a deadly poison.

The rain grows heavier. His voice rises. He makes the point that it is miraculous how people have turned something so deadly into something so delicious. I suppose it must seem like the most distinctive feature of the plant, and therefore its curse, forever labelled as poison and delicacy, removing its presence, erasing its substance.

The seed can be prepared for eating in a number of ways. I believe one of the more traditional methods is to boil the seeds and then bury them with ash, leaving them to ferment for 40 days, a process which leaches them of their poison. I wonder if methods that emphasise boiling affect the flavours that emerge. But whatever it is, he was right. There is something miraculous about it.

I remember the tree, alone in the Gardens, steeped in poison, embracing rain. In a country that adores its milestones, records, and historical narratives, this is a landmark that belongs to me, invisible to others, a corner of my memories, connected to my web of references and remembrances, a network of roots.

VII.

Among the many Agatha Christie books that I rented at Beauty World over the years, I bought a total of five, and only added to this collection when I was older. Eventually, when there was insufficient space on the bookshelves, I think I gave most of them away. I haven't been back to Beauty World in years. I don't think the store is there anymore. I wonder what happened to the middle-aged couple who ran it. I doubt they remember anything about me.

In the same way, I haven't been back to see the tree in a while, and I have also not eaten at a Peranakan restaurant recently. Perhaps I am afraid of being confronted by the formless separation, in touch yet out of reach. They rest better in the realm of memory and narrative. That is, perhaps they live better in the interstitials, out of sight, in my sense of dislocation,

disconnection.

But it is also a dish of celebration, one for special occasions and commemoration.

We are at a more recent birthday celebration. The family has just experienced a traumatic event – the cat has just died – but the meal brings us together. I'm not sure why it is a Peranakan restaurant again. Perhaps it is because my mother was from Melaka, where the culture continues to thrive. To end the meal, buah keluak ice cream, defying expectations.

It is symbolic, playfuil, and almost a little too clever. Yet there is something about the creation of the ice cream that mirrors the ingenuity of buah keluak preparation, as though it displays an understanding of the play of unreadable distance at the heart of my discomfort with the dish. But through the act of reinvention, it keeps alive the connection within me, without seeming like an overused signifier to my cynical self. In it, I see the feelings of connection and exclusion, the overlaps of presence and absence, impossible nearness and absolute distance, ever alive, and ever so close to death. And yet in its playfulness, there is also celebration, reinvention, and healing. I embrace this confusion, this complex condition, drawing closer, pushed apart

my perpetual nausea

There's a Fire at Bangkit

Iain Lim

after I Feel A Fever Coming: A Rengu
Daryl Qilin Yam

I feel the need to plan my breakfast in this country.
A warm plate of bee hoon mee.

That morning I sailed past the Gul beacon.
There's the smell of rust in the evening rain.
Was it a terrible day yesterday?

Dreaming of hash browns & one fried egg,
I always felt absurd, sunburnt and nauseous.

But I did want that last bite,
feeling the sun and wind on your face.
I wanted to write a film about nostalgia.

A very ready dinner,
and the finely minced garlic.

There's new courses to be made,
where the sea swallows the moon.
Is it lunch yet?

I think I need a cup of black coffee.
And pomegranates in tangerine dreams.

Through the thick gloves I feel the barnacles.
It was tea that I wanted.
And what isn't coffee then is coffee now.

I still want to write a film about nostalgia.
The back alley blues, and the dusty ceiling fan.

We haven't fought for anything in the longest time.
The spoons left lonely, and the leftovers.
We can ride the light rail to nowhere for breakfast tomorrow.

I always have dreams.
You can hear them in the gas valves at ten in the morning.

– Bangkit Road, Singapore. 24 April 2016

Lenten Gragoh

Arin Alycia Fong

On Monday I come home to the smell of
gragoh; Nanny is drying prawn paste
by the kitchen window. It smells fishy in the
back bathroom. Like period blood.

Tuesday the entire house smells
like salted fish. Nanny is frying sambal belacan,
the smell of the Straits flooding,
crusting the cabinets with salt and grime.

Wednesday smells like something has
died. Our heads crossed with ash.
Nanny asks what's my sacrifice this Lent
as she beheads a chicken for curry devil.

Thursday's supper is bread and Ribena.
Nanny cleans out the sotong.
Father James washes the altar boys'
feet, among other things.

By Good Friday all smells have died.
I eat a hot cross bun and drag my soles to
church to kiss a statue
of the Lord's bloody feet.

Easter Sunday; sambal sotong in the fridge.
Belacan in jars. The longer you keep the devil,
the tastier it is. I enter the kitchen.
Nanny's already there
like Mary Magdalene weeping
at the tomb.
I smell the sea again.
It has risen.

Comfort Food

Nabilah Said

I went to the market the day after Ma died. My pants dragged unceremoniously on the wet floor. Everyone stared, training their pupils on me. I was a moving target, so I escaped unscathed.

The second day after Ma died, I made a steaming, sweaty broth with some pork bones. My spine, too, felt like it had shriveled up, stripped of marrow and bleached dry. I added the remaining ingredients, watching as the scum rose to the top. I imagined it was my blood, my bile, bitter gall, placenta, platelets and pus, mingled together in a milky film. I let everything fester while I stayed rooted to the darkened spot on the kitchen floor, transfixed by the aching boil.

I opened the lid on the third day after Ma died. The salted veg had caramelised beyond recognition, mirroring my insides. The steam diffused through my pores. I let the stew bubble over till it resembled thick, sopping wet bandages. I tied a long piece of parcel string across my limbs, pulled tight.

Then it was time. Climbing inside, I felt the rush of fluid circulating through my body, my throat, my kidneys, heart, jugular, tear ducts. Thick and salty and warm.

A mother's womb is the safest place to be, I thought, as I closed the lid.

Nasi Lemak

Ann Ang

Calmly licking its chops
the nasi lemak came for me
with the eyes of twenty ikan bilis
like a peacock's tail. Fried lies:
the ikan kuning is crispy and breaks teeth.
Like a virgin moon:
a slice of seeded cucumber
sits amidst
a hand's spread of roasted peanuts.

O the sambal!

Now comes
rice and coconut:
another road from the gas stove,
far enough to be familiar.

Mama's pot is the world.
The same is new and good,
calmly licking its chops.

designer drinks at sub zero

Desmond Kon Zhicheng-Mingdé

to let go, our cupola love of first flares, sudden flax
massive music, beat mixer on three decks

any correspondence reads like a lover's promise
it's possible to say the aubades never mattered

it's possible to be as detached, labels, cold water
because epithets are cheap, effete;

like a good evening out, feigned angst, faux fur
flashcard sommelier when he says it is he who loves

more than everyone else; it is he who doesn't spin
language games; his visions never left tepid

daymark pickle, snivels, yellowing in a jar;
but is this sea chant and table salt?

quizzical himself; the egg has lost its ostrich shell
in vinegar, moon illusion;

show them body armour, what happens anyway
the servile possibility of it, bouguereau in a bounce

“commonplace chirashi frolics...”

Sushiro (now Omoté)

commonplace chirashi frolics and revels withal due respect in finding
the happiness in its simplest and purest form illustrates notably the salt
of the earth praiseworthy salmon and caviar composition is evermore the
kosher desideratum to the epicurean soul.

“sea-water sea urchin coherence...”

Sushiro (now Omoté)

sea-water sea urchin coherence // delectable melange of flavours in cardinal reimaginations of actionable chugalug by seismic rouge waves carrying an abundance of sea urchin gonads onboard an unpresuming japanese sampan leaving every wild inch of japanese culinary footprints in a succinct bite.

"In one's element..."

Sushiro (now Omoté)

In one's element, witnessing the unleash of a sublime creamy collagen-loaded iberico stock as it attempts to befriend and under the one albatross of katame ramen helmed by the ocean's defty gifts and honours to edomae furnishings. this is one of its exquisitely rare sightings.

Tonkotsu vers l'avant.

ARE YOU A DURIAN DREAMING THAT IT IS A POEM, OR ARE YOU

Jack Xi

durians that timelapse back into the rageless cream bells of flowers,
    picked and sold as accessories?
soft batter that does not run hot, amok, and plump in your body
    (instead sliding out without leaving extraneous things like
        weight or joy or fullness in the stomach)?
a durian that smells simple and inedible as white perfume?
a durian that sings as it falls from the branch?
a durian that screams as it falls from the branch?
a durian that farts as it falls from the branch?
a durian yelling *humans smell fucking awful themselves!!*
a macaque brandishing a durian seed on the windshield of your car?
a tree with roots in the pockets of a prehistoric girl's corpse?
a temasek ruler's morningstar, molded after the fury of fruit?
a girl amidst high leaves hurriedly shaving
    the spikes off young durians,
        wishing that deadnames were physical bristles?
a truckful of durians by a truckful of dead bats?
a governmental popup ad for human durian pollinators ?
a thick wriggling insect that secretes itself in durians ?
politicians with small spiky fruits instead of hearts ?
a durian thrown by a political dissident ?
lesbians on a motorbike with durian-shell bras ?
a lovesick mermaid counting husks
    an orang selat woman tossed to the sea ?
a shrine engulfed in trunk,
    devotees braving long months with hard hats ?
an old cishet poet's marriage-bed
    built around the base of a durian tree ?
a durian that catches a coloniser with his pants down ?
ripe alien motifs in a rockatansky wasteland ?

saplings in a macaque latrine deep in bukit timah ?
what raffles vomited, bolting upstairs ?
a durian-scented pack of nippled condoms growing
steadily sweatier in the buyer's hands
the one guy at the orgy with the pungent
hands and garlic lips
the after-durian alcohol your parents
swore would send you straight to hell
origami durians burning, soft in the seventh month wind
poems swaddled in cream and hulls of odorous thorns
a song about extinct fruits on a hovercar stereo
a bissu saint with a spiky, olive-green halo
a 19th century australian man fingering
his distant man's immigrant gift, then
stuffing the long seed in his mouth
before the soil –
a child cutting his foot on his first stinking shell,
not yet imagining any of this

Wild Strawberries

Wong May

That there are such things as wild strawberries!
the old man who sells
potatoes has a small basket of them

That they are wild, he gathered them in the woods
he grows
only potatoes :
I do not know if the potatoes are any
guarantee that the strawberries are wild

But they are good
they taste like BUMBLE BEES
loaded with honey !

So warm
and peppery

from the sun
they charge you

to exclaim from

the roof of your mouth : How Crazy

Careful Careless
Life is –
one can almost
afford to live

Dickson Road Famous Kueh Pie Tee

(SINCE 1899)

Tanglin Halt

Yong Shu Hoong

I'd like to think that the table was wooden
and round and out in the open, to milk
the rustic effect. There is a novelty
in almost everything, when you're below
a certain age – like the plate of pork chops
and fries, so unlike what Grandmother cooked
at home. But I halt myself before memories
fully crystallise – and what is it exactly
that I'm trying to remember anyway:
the taste of salt upon the tip of my tongue,
the atmosphere? I strive to imagine
the helplessness of being young and poor
and open, wide-eyed, to the generosity
of aunts and uncles. This is when my mind
begins to wander – to what film we'd caught
just before dinner at hawker centre.
And right on cue, I remember oily fingers.

A Map of Seletar

Brandon Chew

1. Nim Road (1990)

My first memory is of me at the dining table in the living area of our apartment in Nim Gardens. I'm not sure how old I am – four years-old is my best guess – but I do know that I am eating chicken rice. Chicken rice from Pow Sing in Serangoon Gardens, to this day my favourite chicken rice restaurant. The chicken meat is steamed and not roasted, though any salubrious intentions my parents may have had are lost in a pool of chicken juice and oil of the monosodium-glutamate persuasion.

I'm eating the chicken rice out of brown paper packaging. The rice clumps and mushes between my teeth when I chew. It's definitely lunchtime; the dining room is bright, and the room's whiteness complements the meal's palette.

Nim Gardens is at the end of Nim Road, near Nim Park ('Why waste a good name?' seems to be the motto of developers everywhere). We're as deep in the estate as geographically possible. Beyond the condominium lies an expanse of tall grass; beyond that, Ang Mo Kio Avenue 5, shaded on either side by enormous trees. In the late 2000s, part of this idle land will be flattened for several rows of Stepford-esque terrace housing, connected to the main road but not to the rest of the estate. Nim Gardens will remain.

Not that I know any of this, sitting at the head of the table. Everyone else must have eaten at the restaurant, because all they're doing is staring at me with that typical wonder adults radiate whenever they see a small person do something, as one would a painting in a gallery. *Eating in Miniature. Still Life with Baby and Hainanese Food. Childhood.*

On the left of the table sit my parents, my dad with his John Lennon hair, my mom with her Hubble-size glasses. Are they recording this on tape? Probably – they will record just about everything else I do from the ages zero through fifteen.

On the right sit my paternal grandparents. My grandfather, who will have a series of strokes in the late 1990s and die of one in 2010, wears a kindly smile and a loose-fitting short-sleeve shirt. He's saying something about my appetite and how best to handle me as I grow up. In another childhood memory, I'm kicking his shins in petulance because of some perceived slight. Sometimes I think, irrationally, that this is the cause of his subsequent calamities. My grandmother says nothing. In 2012, she will have a stroke that will render her catatonic and susceptible to pneumonia, which will be what finally kills her six months later. I can't recall which of her many-coloured Peranakan dresses she's wearing.

My maternal grandparents, who aren't in the apartment, live nearby on Jalan Sindor, a five-minute drive away. Go straight up Nim Road, turn right onto Saraca Road, turn left at the end into Seletar Road. Take the right turn at the main junction onto Yio Chu Kang road and follow it until you see a right turn into Jalan Kelulut. Go up, turn left in three hundred or so metres. It's the house at the end. I'm not sure if Ah Ma has already begun to deteriorate.

We're on the eighth floor (or thereabouts) with a good view of the rest of the condo from our balcony. In five years, my security blanket, baby blue and hand sewn by my mother (or bought in a pasar malam), will be thrown down from that same balcony courtesy of my brother, disappearing amongst the grass flanking the pathway to the barbecue pit where I will celebrate my next birthday, and the swimming pool into whose deep end I will be pushed by my father in an attempt to teach me how to swim, a scene made superbly ironic by the fact that my father cannot swim. I will never see the blanket again.

In my mind, my lunch plays on infinite loop. Scenes of great clarity – the food in my mouth, the alabaster of the dining room, my grandfather's smile – repeat over and over. I don't know what happens before or after. The food tastes excellent.

In 1995, we will move out of Nim Gardens and into Neram Crescent, a two-minute drive away. It's more of a pi or a torii in shape than a crescent. Go straight up Nim Road, turn right onto Saraca Road, take the first left where the park is, take the second right.

One day in 2013, my father will convert all his tapes of me to AVIs and play them on his MacBook Air. There I am in the living room: swimming; at my birthday party. My dad laughs at himself laughing at me on tape. My maternal grandmother walks past, still untarnished by illness.

In Nim Gardens, the rice clumps and mushes between my teeth when I chew.

The Nim, or Neem, tree is an evergreen mostly known for its fruit and seeds, which are pressed to obtain nim oil, at times golden, at times brown, at times a brilliant shade of red. The flowers themselves have special significance in certain Hindu festivals; their bitter taste reminds worshippers that one should expect sorrow and happiness, discomfort and peace.

2. Kasai Road/Neram Crescent Park (2001)

I wouldn't call it *a bad date*.

We had lunch at Nooch, a casual-ish noodle cafe in town – my suggestion – well within walking distance of the MRT station. I guess I was hoping for the kind of scenes you see on Channel 5 or at the cinema – boy and girl at a table eating, bonding over some common interest or hobby or something. The magic happens later, but it wouldn't have been possible without what transpired at mealtime, assuming said transpiration takes place to begin with. I'm happy enough that the afternoon didn't end with a tyrannosaur crashing through the windows of the restaurant, or a blue-haired rival lopping her legs off and challenging me to a swordfight – although that might have made things a bit more eventful.

Wait, aren't dates supposed to be evening things? Did I fuck it up, or did she wiggle her way out of dinner? Come to think of it, was it even a date?

In my defence, it's not like I've done this before.

We met in tennis class at Seletar Country Club. It took me at least four Saturdays to talk to her. There had been no ulterior motives, mind you. I was just getting bored waiting in line for my turn to hit a cross-court forehand. She was standing behind me, looking impatient herself, so I thought, why not? Don't ask me what we talked about. Must have been something banal, like racket grips.

Our addresses would have come up at some point, of course. The Club is so geographically removed from anything modern, the only notable landmarks are a swath of colonial-style bungalows, a private airport, and a military camp (ostensibly operational, though the only manoeuvres the men in green seem to be doing are advanced sorties to Jalan Kayu to continue their hungry annexation of the three roti prata restaurants there). The only people crazy enough to invest in membership, surely, would have to be nearby residents; even then, it takes at least fifteen minutes to drive from Seletar Hills to the secluded path leading to the entrance: time better spent taken to get to other, more conveniently located clubs, with bigger golf courses and snootier clientele. My neighbours, all of whom are members – I can see the decals on their cars – must surely have some hermitic blood.

True enough, she lives around the corner from me. Okay, two corners — walk up the slope, turn right onto Neram Crescent, walk for another hundred meters past the park, and that's her house on Kasai. That clinched the deal for me. Anytime we want to meet, we're just a minute away! For weeks, I harboured wistful fantasies of us walking out to the bus stop together on weekends, coming back from a doubles match at the same time, never really being more than two streets away from each other in a forgotten, suburban corner of the island. There are far worse motives.

At Nooch, I ordered the stir-fried beef udon, which was served with minimal aplomb and even less aesthetic appeal. The noodles resembled gigantic maggots in the throes of a wild orgy, oiled up with a peppery sauce and dotted with gobs of red bell pepper. It was an exercise in dignity trying to eat everything without slurping or leaving brown stains around my mouth. There was also the small matter of my poor threshold for spicy food.

Which is why I decided on meeting here at the park for our second date. She once mentioned enjoying taking walks on the circular paths here, surrounded by pong pongs and angsanas and tall grass. "In the park," she said, after burying a most challenging double-handed backhand down the T, "you feel everything melting away with the wind, the world literally miles away." (At least one and a half miles, if by 'the world' you mean the slip road to the Central Expressway). I almost suggested a picnic, perhaps at the meadow farthest from the road, near the corner abutted by the Member of Parliament's house where there *usually* would be no dog poop; but I'd had enough of awkward meals. Best to return to basics, and enjoy the company and conversation.

Wonder why she isn't here yet, though. My text was quite specific about the time and place – I sent it five times, just in case she's having phone reception issues – and I made sure to pick a time when she would be home, right before tennis class.

It's the middle of the afternoon, but the trees shield me from the heat. "Rustle-rustle," go the leaves. She's right – it *is* therapeutic. Maybe this would be the perfect place to talk about *us*, if there even is an *us*. Come to think of it, all I have to do is walk over to her house, ring the doorbell, and ask her to come to the park. She's probably taking a nap, or forgot about it, or something. I'll go once I'm done circling the park. It'll all be cleared up in a minute.

Lunch at Nooch would also have been the perfect place to talk – if I hadn't been constantly washing the sting of the pepper down with water, if I hadn't taken me half a minute and all of my concentration to twirl each slippery strand of udon around my fork before lifting it from the plate, if my predisposition to unhealthy foods hadn't kicked in. I don't remember anything she said. Come to think of it, what did she order? But I do remember wanting to order another plate of udon, which I did the next time I went (with my mother, which meant I was free to pig out in as uncouth a fashion as I wished).

Maybe just one text, to remind her I'm here. No sense in being too aggressive. One text, re-sent every fifteen minutes for the next hour just in case. If there's no reply by then, I can ask her about it at the Club.

Except I will never get to ask her about it. At tennis, she will pretend nothing ever happened. Months later, I will stop going to tennis class (for entirely unrelated reasons, mind you). Over the next ten years, I will have seven girlfriends and go on hundreds of meals with each of them, romantic or otherwise. She will disappear from my life completely, even though a mutual friend tells me she hasn't moved from her house skirting the park. In a neighbourhood awash with trees and narrow roads, it's all too easy to remain out of sight.

In 2008 or so, Nooch will close and disappear forever.

The kasai is a large forest tree than can grow to almost 20 meters tall. Belonging to the maple and lychee family, its fruit is supposed to be extremely sweet, but, like lychee, is difficult to separate from its hard centre.

3. Seletar Road (1995–2004 and 2013)

Getting into Greenwich V, the latest residential-cum-retail clusterfuck to hit the North, from Seletar Hills by car – and you will at some point have to drive there, even if you live nearby, either because you're so deep in the estate it'd take half an hour to walk there, or because you're getting the week's groceries from the Cold Storage – requires a right turn past two lanes of oncoming traffic and enduring more than a few irritated honks from the cars behind you trying to turn up ahead onto to Yio Chu Kang Road. Don't worry. You'll get your revenge when it's their turn to hit the mall next time. We're all neighbours here.

Be careful not to hit any of the illegally parked cars lining the road on your way in. Don't bother with the lots near the entrance to the car park; chances are they're already full. Head straight for the back lots, where incidentally, there used to be an open-air, public car park, right in front of the old Seletar Market. You'll notice that that particular piece of land has been turned into several condominium blocks, the better to bait the ang mohs with. "Conveniently Situated," says the website, "The Undulating Site Has a Serene and Charming Quality That Is Rare in Urban Singapore."

Remember to congratulate those of your friends who decided to buy an apartment. They will soon be living in a quaint anaconda.

Whatever you do, don't think about the old hawker centre that used to stand a stone's throw from where the food court now is; where you spent many a Sunday morning eating (or da bao-ing) bak kut teh (second stall from the right on the second row; do the frail old server a favour and carry your own bowls to the table), chai tow kueh (third stall from the left on the third row; always get the black version, the wok hei really seeps into the radishes), and duck rice (the quality is said to differ depending on which of the two sisters is cooking, but this has not been proven to anyone's satisfaction). The legacy of the place lived on in blobby rings of fat around your digestive system for years.

In 2000, a fire destroyed a large part of the hawker centre and the adjacent wet market, necessitating a massive makeover. It reopened a year later, on the same day the authorities announced that it and the housing blocks on the same tract of land would be demolished and improved, in the name of urban redevelopment and renewal. It officially closed in 2004, many years behind schedule thanks to the protests of the vendors and residents. The ensuing demolition was swift and loud. The bak kut teh people moved to Lorong Ah Soo, the duck sisters, to Jalan Kayu. The whereabouts of the others are unknown.

As if in an act of revenge on the neighbourhood for delaying the redevelopment, the site was allowed to lie empty and undeveloped for over six years, the trees growing around the ghost of a busy enclave, the grass rising tall. Kids would run carefree through the green, teenagers would play the occasional soccer match. It was – what's the word – serene. Charming, even.

Remember when you found out that the developers had finally decided on the project? Remember when you found out what they were going to call it? Greenwich, after the neighbourhood in Manhattan known for its artists and large brownstone houses. You were *living in the actual Greenwich Village* at the time – but you didn't have to be a New Yorker to know that ersatz Greenwich looked nothing like the real deal.

You're here for lunch, but you've quite quickly lost your appetite. It's hard to find anything decent in this palace of plywood and concrete, unless you're into Korean-style fried chicken so fresh it's literally still bleeding, or food court cuisine that puts the 'MMMMM' back in MSG, or shoddy nouveau riche breakfast platters that make you angrier with each bite. There's a half decent design-your-own-ice-cream-and-see-it-man-handled-on-a-stone-slate place on the second floor. The second floor, incidentally, is open-air and features several large tchotchkes that look like benches but are actually water features, because this is 'Village Living'. Help yourself, if you aren't sick of a fad that died out three years ago.

Maybe, just maybe, if you close your eyes, punch yourself in the intestines, and forget about those magical ten or so years of gluttony, the bowls and plates of glop could be almost edible. Undulatingly so.

As you drive out – watch out for the cars again – and turn onto Seletar Road, don't look to your left. There, on the thin patch of land between Greenwich V and the old Singtel building, another developer is erecting a second residential property. Where the McDonald's used to be.

Anyone that demolishes a McDonald's is a fucking monster.

Not a tree. Seletar, or Selita — 'leading to the straits' in Malay — was the name given to a coastal river in 18th century Singapore. It was also used to name the Orang Seletar, a sub-group of the Orang Laut who lived near the river and eventually assimilated into the local Malay population. Historians credit them with contributing to Singapore's eventual development through their trading activities.

4. Neram Crescent (2000)

"Brandon, listen to me."

It's Friday, the only day where school ends before one in the afternoon, which means there was no point spoiling my appetite with a full meal at recess, which means I'm hungry. There's chicken rice for lunch; I can smell the ginger and garlic the moment I get out of the taxi. I'm too busy fantasizing forking pieces of chicken, skin and fat and all, into my mouth to notice the family car parked outside. The gate's already been opened.

"We didn't want to tell you until it happened."

Both my parents are home. My dad is sitting in the kitchen reading a newspaper, his business shirt tucked out and partly unbuttoned. I pray for his sake he hasn't eaten my food.

My mom is standing in the back porch, barking at a short woman I don't recognize. It takes a few seconds for anyone to notice me; when they do, they regard me with detached curiosity, as if wondering why a fat boy has materialized in their living room. Carefully, my dad approaches me. His face looks rehearsed.

"Where's Susan?" I ask. Even if she were upstairs cleaning something, she would've come down by now to watch me guzzle my usual three plates. She's a damn good cook, and she knows it. Chicken rice was the first thing she cooked for us; it's a mystery to me where she got the recipe for it and the countless other dishes that appeared on our table over the past half a year.

That's when they tell me. My dad starts first, with the rueful politeness of someone who's been keeping something secret against his will; my mom, when she's done with whatever she wants to tell the stranger, walks over and interjects. There's too much to process, and their voices meld in my head.

While we were on holiday a few weeks ago, Susan invited a man to the house. "Our house," the collective voice of my parents intones. What had they been up to when we were away? How many times did she have him over? Which of the six rooms – study, bedroom, bedroom, bedroom, master bedroom, guest room – had they been to? What had they done? What had he taken? Moot questions. It was a betrayal of the highest order.

It was Edith who told them. The road we're on slopes downward on either side like a convex lens, and we're at the very bottom. The house on our left is at least two meters above ours, meaning someone in their garden can see straight into our second floor windows, or look down at the study, dining room, and kitchen. No one explains to me how the trespasser was found out. "Thank goodness for busybodies," is all I get. As with all whistle-blowers, there is gratitude tinged with suspicion.

They confronted Susan after I left for school in the morning, telling her to pack her bags immediately. She'd begged for another chance, and, when it was clear she wouldn't get one, a lenient review when the maid agency asked why she was being sent back. Neither was forthcoming. She invited something sinister into our home; she eradicated our sense of safety. These things should only happen in the heart of the city, not in a house miles away from downtown Singapore. Locks will have to be replaced, space reclaimed.

To smoothen the transition, all the arrangements were made in advance, from the termination of the contract to the hiring of a replacement; she's the stranger I saw a few minutes ago. As my parents talk, she sets the table, arranging my cutlery the wrong way because she doesn't know I'm left-handed.

"Susan cooked for you before we sent her off. Go ahead, we've already eaten."

My parents don't ask me how I feel about this. Susan wasn't here for more than a few months. Surely, a fourteen-year-old barely at home wouldn't have been able to form anything more than a cursory relationship with her. True enough, Susan is already slipping from my mind, a candle extinguished by a sudden draft, and nothing seems to have changed. Not even the chicken rice, the only thing left that proves she was ever here.

But what happens after lunch?

A small pot of clear soup bubbles on the stove. It's close to two in the afternoon. I stare out the kitchen window at our exterior wall, which doubles as the foundation of the house next door. Keep your friends close, as they say.

Sometime in 2003, a heavy thunderstorm will cause the drains along Neram Crescent to overflow, flooding our house up to our knees. We will scramble to save the electronics, stacking game consoles and video players on whatever elevated surfaces we can find. My dad will fret over his koi pond; something about pH levels and stress. I will slip and fall into the rainwater. For ever after, the stains on our wooden furniture will remain, faint watermarks reminding us that nature has broken and entered.

> *The neram tree is commonly found near riverbanks, protecting them from erosion during floods. It grows in abundance on the Malaysian Peninsula. If ever they flourished in Singapore, we have since forgotten.*

5. Jalan Sindor (2012)

My maternal grandmother is downstairs for the first time in five years.

Well, not the first time, if you count that fortnight in 2010 when she was shuttled off to intensive care in Tan Tock Seng for fear of another stroke (no one seems to know the exact number); she hadn't had the time nor luxury then to linger in the living room of her own home. I wasn't there when they did it, but I can imagine how much of a chore it would have been to carry her, life support and all, down the floating staircase – pine wood, 21 steps, a ninety-degree turn five steps from the bottom – and into a waiting ambulance. It was much easier this time.

They've put her casket next to the piano and a few feet away from the recliner my grandfather used to prop her up in when she was lucid. Her feet face the front door, her head, the dining room and kitchen. That's about right; she was the de facto cook of the house before the first of the strokes. I didn't get to try her food. By the time I'd reached a formative age, the only parts of her body she could move were her neck and one of her arms.

We're sitting al fresco on plastic chairs on the front porch, listening to the evening's sermon – delivered in Mandarin for the benefit of my grandfather's friends from church. A makeshift pulpit has been set up next to the flimsy tables containing what passes for the evening's dinner. Chicken curry is on the menu. The gravy is watery and the meat – if you're lucky enough to dredge up a nubbin that's more flesh than bone – tastes like rubber.

After the pastor is finished, the eldest male from each generation of the family has a turn. They tell stories from when I hadn't been born, about a woman I never knew. Come Tuesday morning, these men will flank her along with the most strapping members of the cortege, three to a side. They will, on the count of three, hoist her on up and walk several paces to the van that has reversed as close as it can to the house. They will follow her to Mandai, where she will be burned.

For now, audio feedback halts their speech mid-sentence, and the audience covers their ears.

As it is, I'm wracking my brains over the logistics. The front door is less than a meter wide, not one of those grandiose, glass-and-wood-and-gold conversation pieces that decorate the other post-90s bungalows and semi-detached houses along the same stretch of road. Not that my uncles, who still live with their father, were less architecturally ambitious than their nouveau neighbours. Honest businessmen, engineers, the owner of a popular roti prata restaurant chain – they'd inherited hovels and proceeded to replace them with three-storey giants taller than any tree in the area.

Would they try moving her through the floor-to-ceiling windows on the left? Not advisable; the staircase is in the way. How about the patio door on the right? Maybe, but the house is so close to the edges of the property that there may not be enough room to walk. Gross floor area has been maximized, frivolous outdoors spaces eliminated.

One of my grandfather's friends takes the mike. "You want to know what love is?" he asks. "A few years ago, Boon Pin injured his knee and had to walk on crutches. But every night, without fail, he would go up to talk to Siew Chin and keep her company. When I came over and asked how he could do this, he limped over to the staircase, sat down on the highest step he could manage, and used his arms to move himself upstairs, one step at a time. That's love."

Soon after, my grandfather takes the microphone to close out the service. He's lived in this house at the intersection of Jalan Sindor and Jalan Keruing for at least thirty years, more than twenty of which have been spent showering, feeding, and talking to a woman who was physically and mentally wasting away, her speech, sight, and movement shrinking as the houses around her got bigger and bigger, her memories fading as the walls and furniture surrounding her were replaced and refurbished. A year after the renovation, she had to be moved to a guest room on the second floor because there was no space on the first for a hospital bed, and the equipment she needed to stay alive.

"Today would have been our 60th wedding anniversary," my grandfather says, raising his voice to hide the crying. It's the first time I've seen him lose his composure, ever. Almost immediately, he calms down and thanks everyone for coming. "There's still some food left, please help yourselves."

My grandfather had been the one who took over in the kitchen after the illness, cooking not just for the household, but for the extended family every Sunday as well. He had to learn everything on his own, having depended on my grandmother for years. I'm not sure which of the many dishes I've had are his own, and which he adapted from his wife. In food, as in life, the both of them are intertwined. He was going to make chicken curry this weekend.

As the crowd stirs to leave or go back in the house, I think about what my aunt told me on the first day of the wake. "The night before it happened," she said, "we had a problem with the front gate. It just wouldn't close. We had to keep it half-open while we slept. It must have been an omen."

I imagine my grandmother, free at last, walking down those 21 steps. She goes to the bed she used to share, bids goodbye to the man she's spent almost all her waking hours with. Turning away, she walks out the front door through the open gate, into a Jalan Sindor not her own. She picks a direction, takes a few gingerly steps, and then she's gone.

> *The sindora is an evergreen with a wide canopy and prickly, almost tasteless fruit. Many of its species are on the IUCN's list of threatened species, and are in danger of becoming endangered, and, unfortunately, extinct.*

Pantun for a Drink Seller at Newton Circus

Aaron Maniam

'What kind of Indian are you?'
'Apa macam punya mama?' he said.
I had stammering Tamil, two words of Urdu,
It seemed hard to get round his head.

'Apa macam punya mama?' he said.
In Malay, our one common tongue.
It seemed hard to get round his head.
And I shamefully left my head – hung.

In Malay, our one common tongue,
I was tempted to ask, "What of you?
I may shamefully leave my head hung,
But at least I'm not one of the few

Who've abandoned the sarabat-prata tradition
With my stammering Tamil, two words of Urdu,
I'm not the only 'revised Mama edition'.
Just what kind of Indian are you?"

"Besok sunrise egg still put"

Hamid Roslan

Besok sunrise egg still put
inside cup He is aware that Europeans eat their soft-
boiled eggs in cups., correct? Kaya Kaya, or coconut
jam, is made of coconut milk, eggs &
sugar.

can sign petition, sure can – if you stupid
believe sheep can campaign, factory

chicken can Speaker's Corner no permit. His use of the
counterfactual suggests that inanimate objects & farm-
bred animals cannot organise politically. Your heart
so good go debate with their nasi lemak Nasi Lemak is
a fragrant rice dish cooked in coconut milk & pandan
leaf, served with a side of chili paste called sambal, a
hot sauce. lah.

Sambal sure win. Over here your face cry
no use. Will still happy, He will appreciate the bad
food because he has no choice. will still
say thank you.

Even shrimp got brain known when to give up
& kena knife. You haven't.

You write write & write, come back here
want to try sup tulang Sup tulang is made of sheep or
cow bones cooked in a spicy cumin &
chili-infused stew, cooked until the marrow becomes
soft. but when they serve

got no bone. Then bang table. He is angry. Talk
& talk. There is an altercation with the shop-owner. Eh
how you tell me how? He wonders what is to be done.

Sometimes it happens between aisles
in Waitrose. I mistake marmalade for

kaya, think of toast, mouth "nonsense" –
but not alamak. It leaves slowly: trust God

to curse the tongue with groceries. For even
an epiphany needs some state between

betweens. Too pliable the thought, they say,
will end in nothing to eat. Or: trim only

the edges lah. So I trim, am trying, reading
dialect in tea leaves, pretending winter-rain

in England is monsoon season. Presume cheese
is cheese is cheese. Trust only simple nouns –

despite knowing that potpourri has nothing on
rojak. Ridiculous how a radiator tinkers with

air in reverse. How remembering is
an exercise repeated fruitlessly.

A People and a Pie

Tong Jia Han Chloe

We met in December back when I was still in London, at one of those bi-annual potluck parties where too many people brought potato salads but somehow there still wasn't enough to eat.

A mutual acquaintance introduced us, knowing we weren't too far in age and both from Singapore. An undergraduate, he was posted to my company for an industry attachment. He looked vaguely familiar, as if his face was an amalgamation of others I'd grown up with. His haircut that resembled those of other young Singaporean men I knew: short on the sides and completely slicked back on top with a wet-finish pomade.

"Eh, this cake you make one ah? Quite nice sia," he said, crumbs of shortcrust gathering at the corners of his mouth.

"It's a galette," I corrected him, "Kind of like an open-faced pie. And yes, I made it."

"Aiya cake then just say cake la, why need to be so complicated. Simi galette all."

If that was his attempt at a joke, it didn't land. Instead, I felt affronted, like he had overstepped his professional boundaries by speaking to me in Singlish. To suddenly be spoken to in this tongue by someone I had just met felt too personal, too soon. Singlish had been relegated to a small drawer in my mind, only to be pried open during monthly phone calls with my family. Unknowingly, I had dissociated myself from it; let it slip away so I would miss home a little less.

Something similar must have happened to the other bankers, lawyers and professionals that had made their way from my country to the UK, because real, gritty coffee shop Singlish didn't make an appearance even when we were among each other. Oblivious to my reaction, he continued to chew, and the crumbs I had noticed earlier inched closer toward his deep, symmetrical dimples.

Was I being oversensitive? Certainly. But everything I thought I knew about language had been challenged in the last few years since I had relocated. When I arrived in London, I found I had to repeat myself ever so often in conversations to clarify what I meant. Of course, I had expected this to a certain degree; not many in this part of the world had encountered the Singaporean accent and vernacular compared to, say, the Indian, American or Australian.

Still, the misunderstandings arising from my speech bore down on me and I couldn't help but feel the English language was a once fitting coat that had shrunk in the wash. From kindly Indian Uber drivers, I got "your English is very good!", while the policeman who took my statement after a petty theft asked if "English was okay".

So, it made me uncomfortable how at ease he was with himself, this yellow boy in a white place. If I had to be honest, my disapproval of him was really thinly-veiled envy; envy from how he hadn't yet flattened his natural inflections, how he continued to place equal stress on every syllable. When he pronounced my name the way my family did at the end of the evening, I knew I had to see him again. It'd been months since anyone had got it right.

We made our relationship official only after his attachment at the company ended. By then, I had also decided to turn down an extended contract in London, not because I didn't love the city, but because it never came to feel truly mine. Five pounds for a bowl of plain rice in Chinatown on Christmas day? Not my city.

For one of my last meals in the UK, I invited him over to my place for dinner. I thought I did pretty well when I served him a fillet of cod stacked on a bed of baby asparagus and mashed potatoes, but he prodded at the fish curiously and gobbled it down quickly—the way someone might if they hadn't enjoyed the food, but wanted to spare the chef's feelings.

I asked, "Why? Not nice ah?"

I'd begun to felt safe enough in the relationship to speak like I did with my family and really appreciated the efficiency of the language. In fact, it returned to me far more easily than I thought it would.

"No la, not say not nice. Just that I prefer steamed fish, you know? In the broth, with tomato and mushroom that kind."

"Pomfret ah. Means you like the Teochew style la. Walao eh waste my cod."

While he was previously apologetic, his eyes now flashed with excitement. He seemed surprised I knew exactly what he was referring to. My mother was also Teochew, which explained how I knew. Over dessert (which was a fail-proof tub of Ben and Jerry's) we talked about Teochew mueh; how we craved this loose, watery rice porridge rather than the stickier and more popular Cantonese variation easily found in London's Chinatown.

When he asked me if my mother talked loudly and moved her hands excessively when she got excited, all her idiosyncrasies came flooding back to me, as if she'd told me just the day before about a new café she'd discovered down the road. "Is she impatient and short-tempered? A neat freak? The most organised person you know?" he continued to ask, also getting louder and more excitable as we discovered more in common between our parents. His father was the same, and so was everyone else on that side of the family.

If so many Teochews happened to share these 'Type A' personality traits, I understood why they became such successful businessmen and women. Some of my new partner's habits now made sense to me. In his bathroom, all soap and shampoo bottle caps were left up because he felt that having to snap them open and close before and after every shower made for inefficient bathing. He also reveled in doing up spreadsheets for everything, logging anything from petrol expenditure to his term grades at university. On the contrary, seeing numbers in tiny boxes gave me anxiety.

I marveled at how a culture of a people wasn't just found in its food, tradition and art. From our families, we saw how certain traits were woven into the fibers of our being. How curious it was that the specific things I thought made my mother her had come from a legion of people before.

Ga gi nang, he confirmed as I told him more about what she was like, our people. My mother had a habit of saying that whenever she heard of someone else who was also Teochew. The pride and possessiveness that Teochews had over their culture and community made this phrase ubiquitous in their vocabulary: when chatting with a new friend and realising they were Teochew, ga gi nang. When hearing a lick of her dialect in a Chinese restaurant in Sydney, ga gi nang. That handsome rising star on television, ga gi nang.

But I was not ga gi nang. By virtue of patriarchy, I was Hakka like my father, another group from the South of China that was known for their resilience because they were a nomadic people. If Teochews had the richest families in Singapore to their name, Hakkas had Singapore's first Prime Minister as their trump card. Like the rest of my generation, I had that very man to both blame and thank for knowing how to speak English but not my own dialects.

Because I couldn't speak either of my family's languages, I felt abandoned somewhat, denied the richness of my heritage. The earliest words my father spoke to me were in Hakka, and I ate, drank, bathed, pooped with their gentle coaxing. When my mother found out, she made sure the rest of the words I learnt were ones that would get me into university.

My mother may not have taught me the tongue of my ancestors, but she did teach half of what I know about cooking. The other half, Jamie Oliver and Nigella. I suppose deep in the repositories of my mind there was also Martin Yan, who reminds me in times of doubt that if he can cook, so can I.

She joins me in the cramped kitchen and assesses my work-in-progress. "Frozen?" she asks, almost relieved I haven't attempted making the pastry from scratch. You see, in this family there is no shame in the store bought. To the feisty Teochew woman that is my mother, convenience is king, and the glory of making anything by hand is overshadowed by the extra effort needed to clean up afterward.

It is no wonder then that this galette in particular has earned my mother's approval. Thanks to the ready-made dough, it takes only thirty minutes to make from start to finish. We discuss the ease of this recipe and how long it takes, since her own impatience deters her from embarking on any culinary endeavour that requires more than an hour of undivided attention.

She concludes her appraisal of my galette by telling me the exact oven temperature and shelf to use for the quickest bake, and only then do I realise I have forgotten to preheat the oven. Judging by my own haphazard ways in the kitchen, it is clear her meticulousness and efficiency are qualities I did not inherit.

Preparing my galette for the oven, I pinch and fold in the excess inch of dough at the border, covering the outer edges of the apple-fan I made earlier. A brush of egg wash seals the pleats together, and I grate a frozen block of butter over the exposed filling. After a final dusting of cinnamon and brown sugar, the galette is ready.

The following day, I feed him a slice of the galette in his car. He knows by now not to call it a cake. The rest of it sits at home, because bringing the whole tart with me would have made my mother curious about its recipient. I am not ready to answer her questions, just as I am unready to answer his questions about when I will let him meet her. But there is no time to be apprehensive about such things; he is taking me to his favourite seafood restaurant for steamed pomfret, the Teochew way. At my request he has begun teaching me some of the language, the words are still foreign in my mouth. But I am trying to be patient with myself.

At this moment one of his hands is on the wheel and the other in mine. I am content. When he asks me how long it took to make the galette, I smile and tell him the truth—it didn't take long at all.

Kentang

Daren Shiau

labelled by friends as *kentang*, a potato-eater
i struggle with my mother tongue and bungle:
he cannot speak Khek properly
              grandmother tells relatives from the province

her words are like pebbles of uncooked rice
raw and earthy, not softened by heat or tact –
i swallow but cannot digest

i am what i eat, they say

but i know i am not french-fried
though always tongue-tied by Mandarin,
my second language

perhaps, mashed;
quashed by expectations

maybe even a whipped potato,
stirring in milk but also salt to taste;
whisking, whirling

i imagine being a root, dug from the ground
pulled out from these bowels,
no longer soured by cream
but yellow and glistening;
              soaking, whole, in a bowl of curry

The Panasonic

Prasanthi Ram

The Srinivasans were going to America. It was their first trip out of Singapore or India. A two-week mid-December tour from California to Nevada. Mr Chew, their local tour agent, had strongly encouraged them to bring along McDonalds chilli sauce packets; a must-have, he said, for Singaporeans travelling to "angmoh countries". But what truly concerned Amma was that America, with its jumbo hamburgers, lobster rolls and rib-eye steaks, seemed like the last place for a Brahmin family in need of vegetarian options. Especially with Krishnan, eight, and Keerthana, six. They were fussier than she was, even though they and their father were born and bred in Singapore. When Amma asked Appa if there would be vegetarian restaurants in America, he scoffed and said:

"Haven't you seen on TV, Padma? They like their meat. They're proud of it. Those American clients of mine think vegetarians eat grass!"

It was after disappearing into the depths of a Seiyu that Amma returned with an ingenious solution – a brand new portable rice cooker from Panasonic. The cooker was white with tiny orange and yellow flowers, and just large enough for three cups of rice. It was the first item to be packed into their luggage. Soon after, everything else followed, including one jar of Ruchi mango pickles safely hidden in Appa's long sock, a two-kilogram bag of long grain Thai jasmine rice tucked neatly into the cooker, a tin of Milo powder wrapped in Amma's blood-orange shawl, reusable plastic plates and cutlery, a bottle of turmeric, and a small packet of Indian salt because as Amma said, "vellaikaaran salt is not salty enough."

Despite Amma's thoughtful preparations however, their trials began immediately.

On the flight to San Francisco, Appa discovered that the agency had ordered vegetarian meals, not *Indian* vegetarian meals. The whole family gaped at the raw leafy salad tossed with dry pasta, and the dubious sachet of dressing slotted under the cutlery. Bewildered, Keerthana and Krishnan exchanged sideways glances as they stabbed their forks into the leaves in hopes that the meal would magically transform into something more palatable. It was then that Amma reached into her personal tote bag and produced a large orange Tupperware box. The one that she'd been gifted at her first Tupperware party at family friend Anjali Prasad's place three months ago.

Appa groaned. "You brought this even to America? You women are obsessed! What a waste of your husband's hard-earned money!"

Undeterred by his response, Amma opened the airtight lid, revealing hand-mixed curd rice, leftover masala potato, a side of homemade ginger mango pickles and broken papadom sprinkled over the top. Appa had never looked more guiltily grateful as he waited for the Tupperware to be passed down their row, and Amma never smugger.

Then customs happened. Their largest luggage, way over the 30-kilogram weight limit as expected of any Indian family, was opened up by a burly blue-eyed Caucasian officer. In no time, their first offence was discovered. It was the bottle of Ruchi pickles, the one that Amma simply could not leave at home for two weeks. Immigration observed the red oil seeping down the sides of the jar, shook his head, and tossed it. Amma tried her best to look devastated, so as not to let on that she had already packed a backup in Krishnan's Power Rangers trolley bag. Appa lamented in Tamil to the children that a perfectly good sock had to be sacrificed for this smuggling mission now that it had become soiled with pickle juice. But once the rest of the bag was surveyed, they got away with a stern warning about not bringing unopened food items to America in the future, followed by a perfunctory, "Enjoy your stay in America".

It was soon clear though that they would have to improvise more than expected in Ah-meh-ri-ka. Their first lunch in San Francisco was at a Chinese seafood restaurant as the rest of the tour group was Chinese. Concerned, Amma badgered Appa to ask the tour guide about the menu, who then exclaimed:

"Huh, you all don't eat fish ah? I thought Indians eat fish curry a lot one!"

"Fish is an animal, maramandai," Amma muttered, earning the giggles of her children for calling him tree-brained.

For the rest of the day, the Srinivasans were forced to eat pastries from bakeries pointed out by their guide, who now looked at them with constant apprehension. As if their Brahmin presence threatened to overturn his itinerary. By half past four, the family had consumed a nauseating mix of green bean casseroles, pumpkin pies, cinnamon rolls and lemon squares. The only silver lining was finally getting to see the Golden Gate Bridge and taking photos with Appa's disposable Fujifilm, at least until Keerthana puked out her lemon squares all over Appa's leather shoes.

"I want to go home. I miss your food," Keerthana weakly mentioned on the bus back to their hotel as Amma rubbed her tummy with Yu Yee medicated oil. Krishnan echoed his sister while Appa simply sighed from the adjacent seat, staring forlornly at his soiled shoes.

Once they were dropped off at the lobby, Amma yanked a fistful of bills out of Appa's front pocket. He tried to argue over it until she stared him down and demanded to know if he would rather enjoy a decent dinner or be subjected to his daughter's vomit once again. When he predictably conceded, Amma made a beeline for the minimart next door.

She knew exactly what she would be up against, having moved after marriage from Kalakad to Singapore where the nearest fully-stocked Indian provisions store required a thirty-minute drive to Serangoon Road. In the mart, she would not find mustard seeds, urud dal, asafoetida, curry leaves, cumin powder, or cardamom for a good spice fry in vegetable oil. No sambar powder for sambar, no tamarind for rasam, no shredded coconut for avial. No murungakkai or podalangai imported from Tamil Nadu. No cutlery and eating utensils free from the touch of meat or refrigerators untainted by alcohol. No teaspoonful of RKG ghee or cooked dal on white rice for a finishing touch.

Still, she returned in fifteen minutes with a packet of frozen vegetables, a tub of plain yoghurt that turned out to be Greek, and a large packet of original Lays chips that were allegedly saltier than the ones back home (according to a fellow Singaporean family beside them on the bus). Then she got to work.

Dressed down in her long batik night dress and a thick woollen cardigan, she pulled out her prized Panasonic from under a sea of cardigans in the luggage and plugged it into an electric outlet close to the floor. She then measured two cups of washed rice into the cooker, filled it with double the amount of tap water, sprinkled in some salt and turmeric, threw in a cup of thawed corns and peas, and pushed the button to cook. Krishnan and Keerthana, who had regained her appetite soon after her little accident, squatted around the rice cooker in their pasar malam cotton pyjamas. Every few minutes, they took big impatient sniffs of the fragrant steam and giggled at the way it hit their faces if they got too close. Appa on the other hand lounged on the sofa in his white singlet and checkered sarong, legs outstretched over the small coffee table as he watched the same American television shows that aired back home, which for the most part meant Baywatch.

Twenty minutes later, the Panasonic made a slight ding, announcing that dinner was ready.

Shooing the children away, Amma crouched before the cooker and placed four flimsy plastic plates in a row on the carpeted floor. Onto each of them, she served two steaming scoops of steamed vegetable yellow rice, with a dollop of Greek yoghurt that she had watered down for a thinner consistency, a handful of Lays chips and a teaspoon of her favourite Ruchi pickles. Then, in front of the television, the Srinivasans gathered to eat their first proper meal in America. No one complained. Not even when the rice was a little bland without the usual spice fry or pinch of chilli. To Amma's delight, Appa and Krishnan asked for second servings that they ate with more ferocity than the first, and Keerthana licked her plate clean like a starved kitten. In no time, the Panasonic was emptied, scrubbed, and spick and span once again. The family went to bed that night with full bellies and a gentle reminder that home was not a place at all. Home was a feeling that sprung directly out of Amma's masterful loving hands.

From Hungry Ghosts

Koh Jee Leong

My father took me picnicking in Hell
in Tiger Balm Gardens when I turned five.
Horseface and Oxhead flanked the door to quell

tourists, returning ghosts, recaptured live.
Small spectator of retribution's drama,
I shuffled through the dark; I'd rather dive

in and out but the crowd before King Yama
passed as if shackled by the chains of crime.
Father explained to me the law of karma

while a mirror screened a whole lifetime
in a flash. Jostled into Court One, I balked
at heads and arms and legs, in bloody mime,

stuck out from under giant slabs of rock,
impossible to tell which limb belonged
to which gory head on the granite block

(Father said, *Unfilial boys, they wronged*
their parents who gave them everything);
into Court Two where sinners had their tongues

pierced by long knives for lifelong gossipping;
in Three, the greedy were handcuffed and whipped;
the tax evaders, in Court Four, drowning;

one body blurred into another, stripped
of eyes or bowel, heart torn out with a hook,
and on a hill of swords a traitor was flipped.

It wasn't me. It wouldn't be. I shook
as if my bones, and not that man's, were scraped
by sharpeners, for writing a dirty book,

my butt, and not his, by a spear tip raped.
Expecting the worst horror in Court Ten,
I imagined punishments nightmareshaped.

A blue wheel, painted on the back of the den,
displayed the paths for the purged souls' rebirth
as insects, fish, birds, animals or men

depending on each individual's worth.
The worst are born as hungry ghosts, Father said
and strode ahead of me out from the earth.

Under a raintree's shade, he laid out bread,
ham, apple juice. I still didn't feel well.
Eat. Don't waste food, Father said. We fed.

Hungry Ghost

Boey Kim Cheng

Today I saw Granny in Sydney's Chinatown. Her hair pinned and tightly netted in a bun at the back, her arm dangling a rattan shopping basket. She was tugging a boy along in a slow, measured, purposeful waddle. At the combined medical and provisions store on Sussex Street, with a section filled with floor-to-ceiling drawers of herbs and jars of dried and wrinkled tubers and roots, they paused and Granny leaned over the reluctant five-to-eight-year-old and patiently communicated something to him, to make him enter the shop with her. I followed, feigning interest in the vast and strangely soothing store of Chinese remedies.

The voice and language undid the spell for me. Granny was Teochew and loved chatting with the Teochew owner of the Chinese medical shop that we frequented. I would be absorbed, poring over the glass counter in the herb-suffused air and tuning in to the soft mellifluous Teochew sounds, the unhurried friendly exchange between customer and shopkeeper that is no longer possible in this supermarket age.

After putting away the herbal packages in her basket, we would visit the neighbourhood provisions store. Here she would linger over the purchases, ensuring that the owner jot down the right prices as he clicked the abacus and packed the items into brown paper bags. The bags would be delivered by the scrawny young assistant who would later leap to his death from the tenth floor of the block where we lived because of gambling debts. Here was the hub of neighbourhood news. Here you found out about the deaths and births in the neighbourhood: the night before a woman you saw regularly in the shop had jumped from the window of her flat, upon discovering that her husband had cheated on her; there was a gruesome murder in which the victims had been cut up and cooked in curry; a few blocks away a couple had abducted children and killed them in satanic rates; the tiger that had escaped from the zoo had been caught; a python that had been raiding a kampong for its chickens had at last been wrestled into captivity. Here too recipes and remedies were traded.

Last stop: the wet market. It was a tricky business with a five-year-old in tow and lugging a basket of increasing load, and I clung onto Granny for fear of falling on the slimy floor and being left behind. She would poke the pomfrets and the cuts of meat for freshness and haggle and would be oblivious to me and everything else except getting a fresh bargain. She knew the dialect of each stall owner and switched between Hokkien, Teochew and Cantonese, gliding to Pasar Malay when choosing the cocktail of spices from the Indian stalls. Once the basket was weighed with newspaper-wrapped goods, we set sail for home, sometimes with live fish and crabs and often a live fowl, feet trussed up and slung precariously from her basket.

Once home, the groceries would be unloaded and the kitchen work begun. I can see her at her station in life: the kitchen. She had a sad-looking face, the sorrow and worry discernible in her eyes. I remember seeing a picture of her when she was younger, probably in her thirties. In that black-and-white studio portrait, her composed face was tilted to the right, a dignified beauty emanating from the high cheekbones, the beautiful smile and gaze. Now at the altar of the scuffed chopping block, she is all concentration, the sadness gone, wielding blade-work swift and sure, slicing and slivering the ginger and chillies, and mincing the meat with a repertoire of strokes, now a tapping drum-roll, now a regular four beat, smashing the ribs or guillotining the neck of a fowl. She was one of few constants in childhood that you thought would last forever, be always there. Resolutely performing her tasks without a complaint. Mortar and pestle, pounding the belacan, galangal, ginger and tumeric with untiring tempo. It was thrilling to watch; once a headless chicken wriggled free from the chopping block and caused feather-filled mayhem, doing a frenzied tango before expiring in a heap. Another time a crab skipped out of its captive pail unnoticed and was later found alive and well in the toilet cistern.

Between minding the grandchildren, negotiating peace between her children and their spouses, and keeping truce with a truculent daughter-in-law, she managed to cook elaborate meals. Perhaps it was her way of keeping her balance. Certainly, she saw it as her mission in life to feed us, to keep us well nourished. Women of her generation derived their meaning from what they could do for the family. Maybe it was also an impulse, an imperative shaped by the lean times during the war, to make sure we ate well; there was always food on the table, home-cooked food in abundance.

She was disparaging of food from other sources; hawker food wasn't proper food and I don't believe she ever had good comments about the culinary preparations of either friends or her children. It was what she lived for, in a sense, to feed others well, and she didn't miss any opportunity to do so.

Granny was jealous of her culinary responsibilities and secrets. Everyone was banished from the kitchen when she was at work. Once I talked her into letting me slice the potatoes for the chicken curry; at the second potato I was expelled after receiving a rare reprimand for peeling too much off of the flesh. Seldom would she share her secrets, even with her daughters. After Granny's death, the recipes were lost and attempts to recreate any of her dishes fell disastrously short of the remembered standards.

Serving fresh, hot and tasty meals to the family was her daily responsibility and her life hewed to this routine. If she took us out to the shops in town (tua poh or seow poh), or brought us on rare trips to a Chinese kampong in Pasir Panjang to chat with her friends, she would exhibit signs of unease; she would appear distracted, probably rehearsing the recipes while reminiscing about the sua teng days, about friends who had died in the Japanese Occupation. Hurriedly, we would catch the Hock Lee bus back to Toa Payoh, where we lived with Uncle Andrew in the early 1970s. He was the third oldest of her children, after my father, and the kindest and most successful. He was the first in the family to own a car, and would drive us around the island, when his choleric wife was away. Uncle Andrew's problem was being meek and uxorious, he would endure his wife's outbursts against him and Granny without protest.

Granny was stoic about her difficult daughter-in-law and sought to ignore her tantrums and provocations. She found escape in cooking, I think. Unconsciously she was using food as medicine, to assuage the ills that plagued the family.

It did just that during the reunion feasts. All were summoned to the steamboat in the middle of the white marble-topped table (I loved its cool surface with inner ash rivulets). Family altercations were forgotten, dissolved in the steam of the simmering soup. Around it were arrayed plates of fresh prawns, fish, sliced abalone, deli-thin meats, raw vegetables and, each equipped with a copper-wire scoop, we made our selection and dunked it in. The communal cooking and eating from the hot-pout reminded us of our familial bond. It embodied the sense of oikos or jia, the only time when I knew the meaning of the Chinese character for family and home, the roof radical over the pig character.

It lasted hours and people came and went and came back for more, as the simmering soup was replenished. Sometimes my father would show up. One of the tricky things was to arrange the meal such that my parents would not meet. If my mother turned up, which she rarely did, my father would not be there.

There was somebody whose appearance wasn't entirely welcome during the Chinese New year.

The air was immediately strained, the festival mood muted when he appeared, a shrivelled figure, stooped over his walking cane, his thick plastic spectacles overwhelming his sunken face. It took me a while to find out he was Grandpa. This was Granny's husband. We never called him Grandpa. He'd left the family for a fourth wife, who had been a servant, and was never forgiven by my aunts and uncles. He wasn't my dad's father but years later, my dad informed us that Grandpa had died and he was the only one from the family present at the funeral.

Granny was a widow with three children when she became his third wife. My father's father had died, another ghost nobody wanted to talk about. Dad's stepfather kept four households, each wife given a terrace house. By all accounts he prospered after the war, owning a fleet of cargo barges that plied between Singapore and Indonesia. That is until the Konfrontasi, when the fleet lay idle and he went bankrupt. Granny's house was in Irrawaddy Road, in a lane opposite the no longer existent Hoover Cinema. My aunt says the house was a beautiful blend of Chinese, Malay and colonial styles.

They had to sell the house and move to a flat in Tanglin Halt, one of the first housing estates. Grandpa bought another place for his fourth wife and children and stayed with them. Granny carried on serving the dishes as if nothing had happened. She belonged to the old stock of long-suffering Chinese women who always forgave their cheating or wrongdoing husbands. But he was clearly ashamed, always bowed and leaning on his walking cane, chastened by the weight of the past.

Here, in a household of ten, I was born. My earliest memories are not of my parents but of Granny, her calloused hands holding me, or bouncing me and gently patting my bottom as I lay in the sarong sling spring-suspended from the ceiling. Or lying next to her as she lay on the straw mat after lunch, exploring her mountainous body with tiny hands, shimmying the jade bangle along her forearm. Outside the flat, along the corridor, the Malay boy would be singing his mantra goreng pisang, curry pok, ondeh ondeh, his arms dangling two baskets of snacks, or the ancient Chinese woman would make her rounds with her chee cheong fun; on another floor the ting ting tong man would tinkle his chisel, and somewhere below were the cockle, noodle, and rojak men, itinerant hawkers who have disappeared entirely. I loved the feel of Granny's hands, the swollen knuckles, the calluses, the thick hillock of the mound. Walking my tiny fingers over the gently snoring mountain of her body, I felt I was home and whole as I have not felt since.

In the weeks before Chinese New Year, Granny would trawl the textiles shops for material. I relished the textures of the rolled bolts and bales of silk, cotton and polyester, neatly stacked like the sutra scrolls in a Tibetan temple. In one seamless move, the shop assistant paid out the required length with his long rule, made a show of giving the extra inch, then slide the scissors along the edge and neatly folded the material into a paper bag.

At home, the foot-treadle Singer machine would be uncovered like an altar from its catacomb hold, and the bobbin set up with its spool. Between preparing meals, Granny would be pedalling and aiming the cloth at the needle, tailoring new pyjamas for everybody. The only contribution my sister and I made was to wet the tip of the thread and aim it through the eye of the needle. We stood in anticipation, entranced by the whirring rhythms, the piston action printing the stitches, the pedal powering it all. There would be fittings, trying on the cotton top and bottom, and ensuring we would be newly clad on the eve to usher in the New Year.

Once the pyjamas were done, she would begin work on the New Year treats. In the corridor outside the flat, she would set up her clay stove, feed it charcoal pieces with tongs and coax the flames with a straw fan. Out came the moulds for the goodies. Over a few days, the batches of rolled love letters, pineapple tarts, kole chai and kueh bangket would be packed neatly into old Khong Guan biscuit tins and sealed. These would be dispatched by her children to friends and relatives; enough would be set aside to last the whole celebratory fortnight of the New Year.

We watched and ate. We tried to lend a hand but were kept at arm's length. She was a one-woman show, the conductor, orchestra and score.

Each major festival showcased her culinary skills and knowledge. The Dragon Boat Festival was a time for dumplings and Granny's were unrivalled in their variety and taste. There were the small plain ones, shaped like the five stones we played with, to be dipped in sugar. Then there were Hokkien and Teochew and Cantonese versions, each with its own fillings. And my favourite, the nyonya dumpling, with a slightly sweet touch to counter the saltiness of the meat.

Again the clay stove would be there and a bamboo pole laid across the corridor, from which the dumplings would be hung. While my aunt and sister struggled to fold the bamboo leaves into the right mould, Granny was deftly weaving the leaves into a cup, spooning the glutinous rice on and adding the pork-chestnut-mushroom centre, topping it with more rice and wrapping and fastening it with raffia string. All in one seamless motion.

Then it was all dunked in simmering water for hours before being taken out in batches. It was the moment we waited for, to unravel the string, unwrap the leaves and see that gleaming pyramid inviting the first bite.

And in the Hungry Ghost month, when the gates of hell are flung open for ghosts to roam the earth, Granny took us to the Teochew wayang or street opera. After laying out a feast for the dead on the table at home, she would bring us to the marketplace, where a wooden stage was set up and the small ensemble sat tuning their instruments while the troupe applied their last make-up touches behind the backdrop.

On the wooden stage, they acted out stories which we'd seen on TV. (Teochew operas were a regular fare on Radio Television Singapore before the inception of the Speak Mandarin campaign; Granny's favourite opera actress-singer was Tan Chor Hui, who often took on male roles.) I was fascinated by the garishly painted faces, the bright scintillating costumes, the tiered and plumed headgear, the long trailing sleeves, the bobbing flags bedecking the generals' backs. We understood the gestures – the walking round and round denoting a long journey, the martial gesture conjuring up an army. There was, as Shakespeare puts it in the prologue of Henry V, a lot of imagination required. When the action called for a horse, a feathery whip was passed from behind the backdrop – a hobbyhorse without the head. The music would rise to a feverish clanging of cymbals and viols with the duels, the actors wielding and whirring swords and spears, and the villains fleeing backstage as the hero reclaimed his place in history and onstage.

The painted backdrop, which changed with each act, screened off the backstage, where the actors changed roles and costumes, chatted and ate dinner. The minimal orchestra kept the accompaniment going in the wings, upping the tempo with cymbals, lute, as the action mounted into a crescendo.

The audience milled around, staying clear of the front row where the phantom spectators sat. On the periphery were the itinerant hawkers, chiaroscuro-lit by kerosene lamps: the malt sugar seller, the rojak stall, the ting ting tong man, popiah, roasted chestnuts, the bird's nest drink seller.

Granny would buy us malt sugar sticks and we would savour them while she followed the action on the stage, perfectly attuned to the high-pitched Teochew words and lilting melodrama, called home to a world which it never occurred to me to ask her about, a past she never shared with anybody.

Granny was a temple-goer. She wasn't devout or committed like most of her friends, who had an altar with a favoured deity and an urn of smoking incense installed. But she believed in the efficacy of temple visits.

At the Tua Pek Kong temple in Balestier, there were cages of sparrows for sale. The man reached into the cages and grabbed a few helpless birds and transferred them to a brown paper bag. The birds would be set free after prayers, the good deed hopefully increasing our credit with the gods.

She prayed for her children to wise up, for the family feuds to cease, for us to prosper in school. As the exams drew near, she would procure talismans from the temple medium. We would queue for our turn with the intermediary between the gods and man. The woman would listen with eyes closed, as Granny recited her sorrows or requests. I watched sceptically as the medium did a kind of arithmetic with her fingers, and wrote out a panacea with a brush in red ink. The yellow strip of paper would be folded like origami, to be burnt and consumed on the day of the exams.

At Qing Ming, I would assist Granny at the rituals. It was the Chinese equivalent of Ash Wednesday, when we prayed to and for the dead. Like acolytes we held candles like big paddle-pops which we planted in the ground in front of the flats. Then we fed the paper money folded like ingots into the flames, too fascinated by the way the money curled up and translated into floating bits of ash to remember uttering the prayers for the dead.

Later, in her decline, she was persuaded to turn her back on these gods who had failed her and convert to Catholicism. By then she was rendered incoherent by a few strokes and dementia, and it was difficult to know if she understood what that conversion meant.

The day she lost her position at the stove, my grandmother lost her grip on reason and life. She was no longer the matriarch, exiled from her proper realm. The family too fell apart, the reunion dinners ceased.

I saw her for the last time when I returned from Australia for Dad's funeral. Unwanted by her children in her last years, Granny ended up with my sister. We never told her about my father's death. Although Dad disappointed and hurt her the most, she had never stopped worrying about him, always convincing his siblings to take him in or bail him out with loans.

She had stopped asking about him as she slid into dementia. Her mind was erased of memories, almost a blank, though in that sorrowful face you felt she was still there, just out of reach. Somehow in her glazed look I felt she knew.

Now it is almost Chinese New Year. My wife is resurrecting dishes, dredging up recipes from memory, unravelling the ingredients and the steps for our "reunion" dinner. It will be a modest meal, compared to what my wife had back home, and what I experienced in childhood. Just the four of us, no relatives to reflect the reunion nature of the meal. The steamboat will sit in the middle, its rich broth simmering. Around it will be small plates of peeled prawns, sliced abalone, fish, slivers of beef and pork. I see Granny in heaven, calling us to a reunion, her dishes arrayed on a big marble-top table: fish-head curry, pork cutlets with potatoes in soy sauce, nyonya chicken curry, lotus root soup, sambal prawns, lo bak, all the flavours of home-cooking to make us whole again.

As if They'd Been Waiting

Theophilus Kwek

It happened again today. By the time you brought grandma home
she was tired, blue, and late for her birthday dinner. We had her
dressed, then driven to the swimming-club, where fifth uncle had
booked a table. I left you to make apologies while I led grandma
to her seat; she began to spin the revolving dais as if looking for
something. We filled the empty spaces on her left: you were windswept,
I was underdressed. I rubbed your hand under the table, meaning
to say thanks. Then the first three courses came, all at once, as if
they'd been waiting for us. We passed them around in silence. Grandma
took one slice of fish in a spoonful of broth and pushed it in circles;
I thought she'd forgotten how to eat it. But third aunt started a
conversation and I had to turn away. At the end of the fifth course
it was still there, played into a whirlwind by Grandma's chopsticks,
cacophonous: its steamed white lit the long way into the night.

I wasn't sure if Grandma ate it, eventually. I scooped some rice into
her bowl, and then the broccoli. Forgot, then remembered, that she
couldn't eat meat. You shot me a disapproving look. We made
small talk. Everyone's voices wrapped around Grandma, weaving
her wordlessly in. I began to imagine our world spinning past her,
transparent, and she sitting on its tangent, tuneless. She dangled
her legs off the edge of that line, the way we did at that cliff
along the Gold Coast on our holiday. So many years ago: on our
honeymoon or something. I can't remember. You unveiled the cake,
pandan – which Grandma liked – and clapped your hands for
everyone's attention. We sang, passed Grandma our presents,
posed for a picture; sent her home. I drove. You slept in the back.
out of the darkened window Grandma looked uncertainly
for the sky. Then asked, quite timidly, *what was my name?*

Food Preoccupations

Sreedhevi Iyer

If there was a name to define borderline unhealthy preoccupation with food in a Diagnostic and Statistical Manual of Mental Disorders, it would be mine. This preoccupation can range from discovering that rare ingredient that transforms your dish into your mother's, to the 'party food star' fantasy, where your dish is the central celebrity at a gathering of any number of people.

But first things first – so what's your moment, when you're on foreign soil, and you're craving something deeply? When you try to replicate something in that exact way you remember from your childhood. When you stay in denial that it is just plainly impossible.

My moment is tied up with satay. It becomes calcified when I step into a Coles or a Woolworths in Australia, and see jars upon jars, rows upon rows, of pastes and sauces and marinades that boast of ensuring the authentic Malaysian satay experience. It gains momentum when I see perfectly respectable restaurants extol satay on the menu but end up giving you a cross between a barbecued kebab and diluted peanut butter. Thai restaurants seem to have particular expertise at this, as do some Chinese and Vietnamese ones – to lay out a hodge-podge horror of meat pieces on a stick and gaining profit from a falsehood meted out to their customers, like some kind of postcolonial punishment. Most of these specimens are superlarge, dry, and served with an over-rich peanut sauce criminally poured over the pieces. And don't get me started on serving it on top of rice.

I have on several occasions attempted to make satay by myself, at home. I'll show them, I think to myself, although who 'they' were remained strangely mysterious. It had to be done just right, the way I remembered from the *pasar malams* of my childhood. The *pasar malams* were a weekly fix in those days before shopping malls. You knew which markets were on where, which days, and for how long. You went to them because the house needed vegetables, or because you could find those little things you found nowhere else but were absolutely essential to a life of sanity. Like pink rubber doorstoppers, or metallic earwax removers. But mostly, of course, you went because of the street food you would help carry home – it was really the point of the whole trip. And the satay was the king of street food, partly because it was portable, standing in vertical bunches in its bag, and partly because it was something one would never think to make at home, precisely because it was a time-consuming endeavour. Satay was strictly 'outside food', indescribably delicious and tender, and many an excuse was concocted over the years to justify trips to the *pasar malam*.

The very fact that I attempted to make real satay in the comforts of my foreign kitchen, should be indication enough of how much I missed it, and the lengths I was willing to go to for my so-called revenge.

First, I picked Betty Saw's recipe from The Complete Malaysian Cookbook. An everlasting classic, I was told. I was not going to go with any YouTube videos or internet recipes for this one. It had to be from a verified source, historic and dependable. I had to put aside a day and a half to get the first batch out. And really, you never so deeply feel your migranthood, an alien square squeezing yourself into a round hole, as when making your childhood favourite in an Australian landscape.

There were the ingredients. Candlenuts, for one, which had to be ground for the sauce (yes, it's not just peanuts. Peanut butter as a potential replacement drives me nuts. Pun intended). Candlenuts are hard to find, and expensive. As are fresh lemongrass, fresh tumeric, galangal, and shallots. Even by Chinatown prices, they can pile up. But you go for it anyway, because that's how much you want to taste it now, after having found Betty Saw's detailed recipe and the mouthwatering, gastropornographic photograph accompanying it. So you throw yourself into the labour of it, doing things you never thought you would in a kitchen, like soaking bamboo sticks overnight. Even my grandmother didn't soak bamboo sticks.

You chop, you slice, you grind, you steep. You stink up the place frying *belacan*, you scream in pain after wiping your eyes with chilli-stained hands. And finally the sticks with marinated pieces of chicken are ready for cooking.

Now, do they go in an oven grill, or a stovetop one? Perhaps a coal-fire barbecue is the closest? The rest of the preparation is followed closely, including the spiced peanut sauce with the consistency of a cream of mushroom soup, chopped cucumber, and *ketupat lontong*, steamed rice cakes.

And yet, there is something missing. An absence persists on your palette from first bite to last. Had there been too much basting, or perhaps too little? Was it not sweet enough, spicy enough, tender enough? It was probably the cooking implements – even a charcoal barbecue could not compare with the metal contraption set up under the *pasar malam* tent, with billows of fragrant smoke acting as the perfect advertisement throughout the bazaar. Yes, that's what it was – the smokiness, the charredness of a memory stuck within the confines of a lost time. I had to admit defeat. The real satay of my childhood remained there, and there was no way I was going to be able to recreate it in my ill-equipped kitchen. I was going to have to suck it and shell out big bucks at bigger restaurants for something I used to take for granted when I was ten-years-old, and then pray some Michelin-aspiring sous chef at the back had been to Malaysia and knew how to get it right in his stainless steel industrial kitchen. So much for revenge. I threw Betty Saw's *The Complete Malaysian Cookbook* in the bin.

And this is the thing people like us, living overseas, have to live with, whether we like it or not. Real or otherwise, our cultural food is crucial to our health, but not in the way that omega 3 is good for your Alzheimer's. It affects moods on a slightly misanthropic level. I can never go two days, for example, without something spicy – it is integral to what I consider adequate nourishment, basically a whole food group. In Australia, it has developed into an overpowering neurosis. I take my own personal chilli sauce to roast lunches at work. It is a delightful little bottle, half the height of your average Maggi, that I found at a spice shop. "Travel size," I'd say to my colleagues at the table, drawing concerned looks. It doesn't end there – obviously the right kind of spice and heat is also crucial. I have 12 different kinds of chilli sauces in my pantry cupboard, and sometimes none of them are what I'm seeking. I recently bought my thirteenth, a pineapple chilli sauce. It has a thin pour and a very unique zing, and I'm still trying to find the right occasion to fit that in. People don't seem to understand this, but the right food makes all the difference. I pilgrimage to outer city enclaves for a good *roti canai* when I'm particularly disenchanted at the workplace, because *roti canai* is the typical worker's breakfast. I always remember the simple humility of honest work that the *mamak* migrants do back home. And something as innocuous as a curry puff can get me depressed, because it was the ubiquitous snack in my primary school. It had been ever-present at tragically uncool class parties chaperoned by bored teachers, and had been the cheapest purchase at recess in the school canteen. This then publicly and irrevocably damned the buyer, because it revealed their social class.

So whether we like it or not, food is more than a nostalgic conduit to a lost homeland – it is also incredibly relevant to our everyday sanity.

If I had children, then, the preoccupation might take on worrying proportions. What do you do with kids growing up in the Australian cultural climate? Thanks to the global village and the Internet and academic terms like diaspora, I now know that despite my own curiosities, I will instantly and miraculously transform into the straitjacketed, traditional ethnic mother that all second-generation Asian-Australian children love to hate. I will become one of those who habitually insist on the tried and true methods of pan-Asian parenting, such as expectation of high grades, unquestioning obedience, and most of all, that greatest gift that only the Asian parent can give, the passing on of cultural legacy. And given that it had earlier been established that we possess an unhealthy obsession with our food, it is now obvious that such cultural legacy would take the form of meticulous preparation of elaborate dishes with equally elaborate names that only people like David Thompson and Matt Preston may have even heard of. And if the children were truly lucky they'd be repeatedly lectured on the particular historical origins of these dishes, too, like the korma. I would suddenly want them to know and understand that it was originally called Quarama, due to the Persian influence in South and Southeast Asia, and that the *roti canai*, which it goes very well with, is a corruption of the word Chennai, the old then new name for Madras in Tamil Nadu, although really the *roti* itself came from the Malabar Muslims of Kerala and is rightfully known as Malabari *paratha* in that region. And I would of course not want them to have fallen asleep by now.

But if I wanted to be a really cool parent I am going to have to up the ante. No, not in the way you think. I'm not talking of Australian food adjustment – that is now a given. A friend of mine once told me of her son who came home from school with his lunch of chutney sandwiches still intact, because his friends called them "poo sandwiches". He didn't want them anymore. My friend now makes him what he calls "regular sandwiches", which she cannot bear to have herself since they were tasteless. She's from Delhi, and she thinks maybe at the next play date she may make chutney sandwiches for the mothers, too, just to expose them to something more interesting, and that might stop the jibes. I told her she ain't seen nothing yet. (I also saw the beginnings of the "party food star" fantasy).

But this Aussie food thing is no longer scary, not even remotely. I'm not talking about bemoaning the fate of my children as I acquiesce to making beef burgers on the grill, or turkey sandwiches for school lunches, or even colouring hard -boiled eggs. The last, I admit, is something one has to concede to at Easter just as one would surely have a giant Christmas tree every December, and then wonder how to navigate through the living room, or trying to figure out its relevance to Australians down under in the summer, much less your own family. No, these kind of adjustments, which actually help children form their identity in the new country (or actually confuse it even more beyond recognition, I can't decide which), these I can live with. No, I'm talking of bigger challenges.

I now live in a world where MasterChef, irrespective of season, is now a perennial entry in the top ten list of most-watched television shows in Australia. Everyone watches them. They even watch the celebrity and junior versions. Chefs go on talk shows, the judges get books out, and suddenly everyone is boasting about what they made for dinner last night, and how their cousin's *tarte tatin* was just okay. Overnight, we have become gourmets. And because of climate change, suddenly we're not just gourmets, we're gourmets who are environmentally conscious. You don't just make your own food, you now have to freakin' grow it yourself. You have to find soil, fertiliser, and sapling, and then you have to water, not water, nurture, prune, check the soil, check the sun, check the humidity, check the season, and then you may eventually be rewarded with a harvest that will last two minutes before you chuck it into a saucepan. And on top of it, it all has to be sustainable, whatever that really means.

My as yet unborn children are going to be expecting all this – especially since by the time they're old enough to watch television the kids of Junior Masterchef would have grown up and might possibly be hosting more extreme versions of the show, exerting even greater pressure on their nutritionally-aware selves. I am going to have to go to farms with my children. I am going to have to watch cows getting milked naturally, perhaps even do it myself, and pretend it's great fun. I am going to have to spend a fortune buying the organic version of everything, from onions to spaghetti to crisps. I'm a little unclear as to how the last one works, and people seem to confuse the 'organic' label on crisps with 'low-fat', which isn't the same thing, and low-fat doesn't always mean low-fat anyway, because of the sugar content. See, I digress, and I'm going to have to know all this, not to ensure my children's health, but to ensure my pride when they quiz me at the dinner table after acing a test on it at school. I'm already longing for a processed, carb-laden, eighty-percent-sugar snack just thinking about it.

I understand how all of this is very very important to the planet, but you see, I come from a generation that has already seen this. I grew up with wet markets of stinky fish and rotting vegetables (which must have been organic but nobody mentioned anything because back then that was just normal). I am from the time and place that Luke Nguyen creepily idolises in his television shows, the forgotten pre-modern spots that people like Nguyen exoticise, sounding more like a foreign tourist guide rather than a returning exile fully aware of why his surroundings are so different from his audience's. I remember a five kilometre queue outside the very first Kentucky Fried Chicken outlet when it first opened in my sleepy hometown, as much as I remember the *pasar malam* satay, and I clearly knew which was the cooler thing then, just as I know its opposite is cooler now. Back then, we welcomed Kraft slices with open arms. We were overjoyed with canned baked beans. Someone brought a spongy baked cheesecake to an outdoor dinner party and served it in little squares, and it was the absolute star of the event (you can see where I get that fantasy from). So I basically worshipped at the altar of the Goddess of Process, and then when I came to Australia, I very understandably went completely mad. Until I missed everything that I had taken for granted at home.

So this is full circle. To raise my still non-existent children, I pretty much have to convince myself that all the advancement of civilisation in Australia, for which I had given up a home country and had merrily made myself a migrant, was a fallacy, and that I had to revert to a way of life that is truthfully quite agricultural, which means my forefathers in Asia had been right all along. And I have to do it to ensure my own progeny, who will never know a culture other than one drastically different from their parents', will grow up with all the food values that I myself considered seriously outdated in a progressive society. I have to turn on my own chalked-out food trail into the unknown, and teach my next generation what I disbelieved in. Yes, it's for the planet, and for health, but it's also a demand too great a magnitude to bear sometimes.

Still, I'm hoping I will finally bring that dish that will be the star of the party. Preoccupations die hard.

Mango

Shirley Geok-lin Lim

A mango at the New York A. & P.
at eighty-nine American cents each,
heaped by apples: a stony red, puffy
hybrid all the way from Acapulco,
from corporate farms and rich Yankee
enterprises.
Then two days later,
Older Brother slowly drives me, Straits-born,
home through narrow, rewritten Malacca.
Before broken Chinese houses whose sons
and grandsons have left for Australia,
umbrella trees drop welcome shade.
Crescent mangoes like smooth-thighed trailer-
girls from Siam gleam among sickle-drawn
leaves.
I eat a green mango. Solid,
sour, it cuts the back of the throat, torn
taste, like love grown difficult or separate.
More chilies, more salt, more sugar,
more black soy – a memory of tart
unripeness sweetened by necessities.

Where do we go from here, carrying
those sad eyes under the mango trees,
with our sauces, our petty hauntings?

Love Poem to Jollibee

Rodrigo Dela Peña, Jr.

dear bee waggling from city to homesick
honeycomb city

with your chickenjoy your whoop-inducing
sweet spaghetti

for you i am willing to stand in a queue
like a true blue

singaporean & for you i endure
assorted portmanteaus

like crispylicious juicylicious
all the blunted

exclamations approximating
the thing itself

o fast food fantastic under your halogen
lights i am a wide-

eyed child once again dipping crisscut fries
in a nautilus swirl

of strawberry sundae & can i have a peach
mango pie please

plus a regular yum with cheese
beloved bee erased

of your sting you buzz variations on the theme
of home and home and home

How do you want your dumplings?

Anitha Devi Pillai

We sat silent for far longer than I could bear at my parents' flat in Bukit Panjang.

I studied the man in front of me in his salmon-pink Ralph Lauren shirt and beige pants. His clean-shaven face was missing the characteristic thick moustache that my uncles and cousins in Kerala wore as the symbol of ultimate manhood. Apart from his name, Kunthatha Veetil Shakthi Menon (aka K V Shakthi Menon), there was very little to give away the fact that he was born and bred in India.

"Do you want to get out of here?" I asked hoping that perhaps he would open up once we were out of the watchful eyes of our parents and relatives. While our families seemed to be engaged in their own conversation about the well-being of relatives in Kerala, I could have sworn that all ears were, in fact, straining to hear our conversation.

"Yes," came the swift reply. "Is there an Indian place around here? I'm starved for Indian food." His heavily American-accented speech bore no traces of his Indian roots.

We made our way to the ground floor of my parents' flat where there were three coffee shops, a wet market, two bakeries and even two mini-marts. The amenities had been the biggest draw for my parents when they bought the place.

My mother was elated to finally move into a flat that allowed her to whip up her meals in a jiffy. She could pick up a crispy deep-fried spring chicken from Heng's BBQ and Fried Chicken store, two or three vegetable dishes from the Malay or Chinese stores and spicy fish curry from the Indian store. She cooked the rice at home, of course – one could not get the *Palakkadan Matta* rice from Kerala at the coffee shops. The rice was supposed to be the healthiest and had its own unique flavour that my father loved. My mother didn't care too much for it, but it made her husband happy as it reminded him of his mother's cooking.

On days that she felt like she wanted to cook the meals 'from scratch', she got the Indian Muslim stallholder at the coffee shop to make her fresh paratha and to chop it up on the *tava*. Returning home, all she had to do was to dice the onions and large green chilies, fry the minced lamb with House Brand Curry Powder's all-purpose curry masala, add an egg and finally toss in the paratha. And, lo and behold, it became *kothu* paratha! It only took her twenty minutes to cook and that was her idea of a truly home-cooked meal.

I picked the store that had the best Indian food and got Shakti seated at the far end of the coffee shop.

"*Anneh*, two *mee goreng merah*."

"*Urappu koode podunga*," I added in Tamil remembering that Shakti had mentioned wanting something hot and spicy.

The stallholder pointed to the items on display that were meant for Indian rojak and waited for me to tell him if I wanted any extras added to my dish. I picked out a boiled egg, fried fish cake and fried tofu and raised my finger to indicate that I only wanted those extras for one mee goreng dish.

"One vegetarian and one with these," I added, just to be sure that he got the message.

I stood there watching the stallholder throwing the yellow noodles into the wok and dousing it with his special mixture of tomato sauce and sambal chili that gave it the distinctive red colour. He added additional green chilies as I had asked for mine to be made extra hot.

My thoughts drifted back to 'the stranger' waiting for me at the table. If all goes well, in a few months, he would no longer be one – in fact, I would have been married to him.

It was not a particularly unusual arrangement. From what I gathered, my great- uncle, Kizhaku Veetil Lawyer Gopalakrishan Nair, had run into Kunthatha Veetil Engineer Gopalakrishan Menon at the tea shop one lazy evening in my ancestral village town, Ottapalam, in Kerala. There were so many Gopalakrishnans or Gopal Krishnans in the Malayalee community that they were often referred to by their jobs despite having long names that included their ancestral home names and caste names that distinguished them.

As destiny would have it, the conversation that afternoon at the tea shop turned to family members who were of marriageable age.

Engineer Gopalakrishnan lamented that all the offspring in his ancestral home, Kunthatha Veedu, were born with a '*naga dosham*' or the 'curse of the serpent', according to their horoscopes. Legend has it that one of their servants had poured hot water into the outhouse during the wee hours of the morning. It was their daily routine to do so. The servant had not noticed the two entwined cobras that lay at the entrance of the outhouse. The snakes died. Despite the family not being superstitious, they could not explain why after that incident, all the offspring who traced their roots to the Kunthatha Veedu were born with the 'curse of the serpent' in their horoscope. And the astrologers never failed to remind the family that they could therefore only marry someone who had a similar curse in their horoscope.

"So you know how it is. It is really hard to find someone with a horoscope that matches these children. If you know anyone with such a horoscope, do tell me."

That's when Lawyer Gopalakrishnan remembered his uncle Kizhaku Veetil Pathmanathan Nair, who had moved to Malaya in the early 1900s to teach mathematics at a small school in a rubber estate. Uncle Pathmanathan had a great-grand-daughter in Singapore. From what he had heard, she too had some sort of 'a tainted horoscope'.

"Aah, she will be suitable for our Shakti. He is too good, I tell you. He is thirty years old and works as a computer engineer in the US. He completed his Masters at MIT. Now the fellow is a team leader, drives a big Camry car and even has his own three-bedroom flat in a good area in Louisville. You know, Kentucky?"

That conversation might have happened by pure chance but things moved like clockwork after that. The two Gopalakrishnans headed off to Astrologer Attukal Raman Panicker's home, armed with the horoscope of the 'boy' and 'girl'. Astrologer Panicker looked up at them with a smile after studying the horoscopes for what seemed to be an incredibly long time. That meant that it was a good match. Only then did both Gopalakrishnans heave a sigh of relief in unison.

Phone calls were made to the respective parents. The 'boy's' parents in Delhi were urged to instruct their son to travel to Singapore. Photographs and detailed biodata – which even included hobbies – were exchanged. The Gopalakrishnans reminded the parents of how difficult it was to find someone suitable, and, if either of them chose not to marry someone with a similar horoscope, the marriage was doomed to fail and, in the worst case scenario, they would end up widowed. When both families raised no objections, the 'boy', Shakti, made the twenty-four-hour trip to Singapore from Louisville the following weekend.

I returned to the table, gingerly holding in both hands the plates of hot *mee goreng*. I placed the one that was laden with all the extra yummy ingredients in front of him.

"Here! Eat it while it's hot. It's the best Indian food in Bukit Panjang!

"Indian food? How is this Indian?"

I could have kicked myself then. I had not realized that for someone who was raised in India, he was probably looking for the more traditional fare of *idli* and *dosa*, all of which required a forty-minute trip down to Little India from Bukit Panjang.

"Your parents were born here, they said. Is this what you grew up eating?"

"I do eat *dosa* and *idli*, but it is not a regular feature in my home. I should have qualified that *mee goreng*'s claim to fame is really as a ubiquitous Singaporean or Malaysian Indian dish. Mom's not big into the traditional Kerala fare, having been born and raised in Malaysia. Plus, honestly, Shakti, you know Amma is a poet, right, and a strong feminist one to boot? Now that is a code to say that she has no time to cook."

I earned my first smile from him. He poked his fork into the noodles, engrossed in his own thoughts.

"Do you like poetry?" he asked after a few minutes of silence.

I nodded. It was a strange question to ask of a secondary school literature teacher.

"I wandered lonely as a cloud,
That floats on high o'er vales and hills,
When all at once I saw a crowd,
A host, of golden daffodils;
Beside the lake, beneath the trees,
Fluttering and dancing in the breeze."

The last thing I had expected any man to do at the first meeting was to recite a poem by my favourite poet. Quite oblivious to my reaction, he continued speaking.

"I love poetry. But in India, if you are not going to be a doctor, you take the IIT entrance exam. If you don't make the cut for IIT, then you apply for an engineering degree elsewhere. There are no other options. No offence, but folks back home think that literature is reserved for those who can't make it elsewhere."

He placed a piece of fish cake rolled with a few strands of the noodles into his mouth rather cautiously.

"Thulasi, when we retire, let's move to Kolkata and spend the rest of our lives writing poetry and walking down College Street. They call it the biggest book store in the world! Kolkata is the city of poets and writers. You will love it there. Anyway, children in America leave the homes once they are eighteen. When our children leave for college we will be alone in our big house. What do you say?"

I smiled, not just at the sight of his eating the *mee goreng* with a gusto that was rare for a first-timer but also because he had recited Wordsworth, and planned out the rest of our lives in the space of just a few minutes.

Thankfully, I did not have to move to Louisville after our marriage. Fate intervened in the form of Astrologer Attukal Raman Panicker, again, who prophesied that "if the girl were to move across the oceans after marriage, the marriage will end in a divorce!" Of course, the Gopalakrishnans had not thought that they needed to share this information with the families until the marriage was fixed. I was secretly relieved.

Over the next few years I learned the difference between authentic Kerala dishes and the variety that I grew up with in Singapore. Shakti constantly reminded me that the mark of a true Malayalee was to be able to speak the language well and cook the meals right, especially on Onam day. Come every August he would start harping on the same mantra.

"Onam is the most important day of the year. That's when our Maveli King visits us from the underworld. We must wear new clothes, deck the house with flowers and welcome him with a good meal. It's our tradition! We cannot lose our tradition just because we live in Singapore!"

So he took it upon himself to teach me how to make all the twenty-six vegetarian items of the traditional Onam meal or *Onasadya* from scratch. I wasn't a very good student. He had to repeatedly explain that long beans *thoran* had to be well-cooked and soft, rather than slightly crunchy like the ones we got in Singapore. My mother quietly remarked to me that Shakti was "overcooking the vegetables and killing all the nutrients!"

My mother, took to politely declining to eat with Shakti on Onam day, out of respect for her son-in-law. The truth was that my mother would secretly cook her signature mouth-watering dishes – tofu-sambal and *vatha kuzhambu* – both of which were not from Kerala and hide it away in the refrigerator. It was her dishes that packed a punch to the *Onasadya* spread that he cooked. But these dishes only made an appearance once Shakti left the flat.

Alas, my marriage was a short-lived one. I blamed it on the long working hours where "there was no work-life balance". My parents blamed "the fraud Attukal Raman Panicker" for cheating the family for a handsome commission. The Gopalakrishnans and their wives blamed it on my inability to even cook a "proper *Onasadya* to keep the man happy at home!"

The truth was that I had found a handwritten note from a Jaslyn Teo tucked into Shakti's golf shorts one Sunday afternoon.

> "as
> we lie side by side,
> my little breasts become two sharp delightful strutting towers and
> i shove hotly the lovingness of my belly against you ..."

I did not read the rest of the love note. I knew my e. e. cummings well. I clearly did not know my husband. Nor did I want to anymore. I filed for a divorce soon after that and spend a deeply satisfying afternoon burning Shakti's carefully handwritten collection of Kerala recipes over the kitchen sink.

But that, of course, was a long time ago.

Shakti remained the doting father that he had always been, and for that one reason, we remained friends. So when he suggested taking our fourteen-year-old daughter, Jyotsnaa, out to celebrate her being awarded the first prize for the script that she had written for the Book Trailer Competition at the 2017 National Schools Literature Festival, I was all game. In fact, the literature teacher's heart in me was bursting with unspeakable joy at Jyotsnaa's success.

Shakti made reservations at Din Tai Fung, a Michelin star-awarded Chinese restaurant. It was his favorite restaurant these days. He now spotted a bald look and a six-month pregnant stomach that he proudly claimed to be the testament of his new wife's cooking. His Raoul shirt screamed out for a release with his every movement.

At the restaurant, Jyotsnaa and Shakti studied the menu carefully and then ordered the usual: steamed pork dumplings, pork and shrimp dumplings, wanton noodles for themselves and a set of steamed vegetable dumplings for me.

When the dumplings arrived, they picked them up carefully by the tip with a pair of chopsticks, and dipped the dumplings in the bowl of vinegar and sliced ginger. Then they placed the dumpling on their soup spoon. Shakti reminded Jyotsnaa to poke a hole in the dumpling or she might burn her tongue. I watched as both of them patiently waited for the juice in the dumplings to be released onto the spoon before scooping it into their mouths.

Ironically, it was Shakti who had taught Jyotsnaa to use chopsticks as it was the one skill that I had never picked up despite having been born and raised in Singapore. Well, my Chinese friends did not eat their curries and rice with their fingers when they were with me at Indian restaurants, I had reasoned. In any case, all my friends were health nuts who preferred salads.

When my dumplings arrived, I cut a dumpling into halves with my fork and spoon, scooped up generous portions of chili and vinegar and stuffed it into each half of the dumpling. I drooled at the sight of my dumpling soaking in Din Tai Fung's signature chili.

Shakti stared at me with a tinge of amusement and irritation that day. When I placed the dumpling in my mouth, he burst out and exclaimed "Oh God! Thulasi, you are so bloody Indian! Do you have to spoil the taste by adding chili to everything?"

Nenek Taught Me To

Hidhir Razak

fool them
with one worn knife
like cutting half a chicken

into fourteen pieces
on special occasions
or chopping more onions

into three scrambled eggs
to feed thirteen. Give
the older ones less because

the younger ones still cry but
push every scrap of
garlic into their plates smiling.

Piling rice onto your husband's
portion with enough sambal
to silence him cools the temper

like raw cucumber
and sliced apples taste sweeter
sprinkled with salt. Meals end

when tea is served, always sweet
enough to dream on,
then turn off the stove where

fish has been fried till dry
enough to keep on
for tomorrow and tomorrow
and tomorrow.

Garam Assam

Hidhir Razak

A kampung dish. Salt tamarind? Sour salt?
Tamarind for tang, salt to sweeten

Ibu inherited it from her Nenek, who'd detested
her hands, feet, face, and so had taught
under an angry eye
everything she couldn't pass on.

– why bring this Chinese girl in? we don't need her –

and it looks like a curry, from the brown of ground cumin and clove
blades of kaffir slicing through from beneath the slick
beef fat mingling with coconut oil, lemongrass stalk and cinnamon curls
straight as masts without sail

They'd lived by the sea; salt is light as breeze
Ibu learnt to tend to fire from her Nenek, whom she'd wept for
everything; she passed on. The garam softens the masam,
tamarind tears

– her own mother didn't want her, easier to be childless
and poor –

cuts through the fatty blood, brightening the palette. It is a rare find
in malay stalls and restaurants here among the assam pedas, the rendang,
the lemak chili padi; easier to find this dish in Peranakan kitchens, often
cooked with pork.

through salt. Some long-forgotten moyang planted tamarind right
behind the kitchen. The fruits fed many mouths while its branches
tear through the same roof, over and over,

– you were fated to be barren, and I was fated to feed her –

boring a hole through which fell dead leaves, tamarind, rain and light.

– has she eaten? –

five spice

Madeleine Lee

i. clove
– also cengkeh

ostensibly nothing but the dried stalk of once
fuschia blossom of the myrtaceaem tree
which the natives harvested shaking
in the wake of tyrannical botanical history
sneaking out of dutch clutches to africa
on v-o-c passage
carrying jawanese slave cargo to amsterdam
back again to maluku to zanzaibar to madagascar
on the round trip blended with shag tobacco
for that sizzling crackling kretek smoke

ii. coriander
– also ketumbar

a small round seed stowed away
in the mycenaean battleship
as the soldiers readied themselves
for the rout of troy
on land it hid in the store
of the army cook as fires rage
on the battlefield and on his stove

the victors left braying
the seed left fallow
finding home on alien earth
in south west turkey
a taste of asia

the new seeds in jute sacks piled on caravans
of turkish merchants
traversed the steppes crossed the himalaya
ending up in countless curries

iii. cinnamon
– also kayu manis

a cappucino in a japanese café
insists on the accoutrement
of a foil-wrapped stick of cinnamon bark
in place of a teaspoon
as if the mere dip and stir
would impart further headiness
of sweet bark in the hedonistic brew

a sticky bun is so named
because if you cook cinnamon with brown sugar
and applied it on a regular swirling bun
it would cause it to become quite stuck
to your saturday morning hands

iv. cumin
– also jintan putih

from ancient sumeria the gamun
dispersed throughout syria and persia
and found its way into biblical aftertaste
in isaiah old and matthew new
the romans rejecting the teaching
imbibed the pleasures of the tummy calming seeds
if only there was such a simple tasteful solution today

jintan putih and jintan manis
says the solo cook
as she tries to separate the two types
previously thrown together thoughtlessly
into the same plastic tupperware

jintan putih the brown rat hair like one is fennel
jintan manis the green rice grain sized one is cumin

after a solidifying meal
of chicken masala and pilau basmati
there is delight in the partaking
of the breath freshening pinch
of cumin and colourful sugar beads

back then my father carried on him
a small tin box of jintan to be chewed
a few at a time as an after-dinner digestif
nowadays he has taken to asking for
a replenishment of jintan hitam liquorice candy

the french preferred theirs
yellow-green and overly alcoholic
sitting round the iced water canister
watching the drip drip drip

v. cardamom
– also kapulaga

instead the cardamom chose a buddhist trail
from india to bhutan to nepal to burma to ceylon
its parakeet green bead marked by a saffron tip
as if the monks' robes rubbed off on them
as if the noble truths had

gulab jamun

Wahid Al Mamun

these days ma gets her gulab jamun storebought from the mustafa frozen foods section airpacked in one of those twentyabox types she had misplaced the family recipe years ago at a customs desk from dhaka to singapore so this is the easiest way to dig for cultural loot locked beneath the brown flesh that gives way to spoon's spade. even in processed form there is a rich hint of almonds and rosewater for the coating or is it cardamon? crucially ma

can't seem to remember. the coating tastes like rust so we stop working our way to memory from taste backwards on this pretext but i know ma knows that the brown flesh held the secrets to a past life in mirpur road sweetshops the best in the world she once told me where there were trays upon trays of boisterous flavor paraded like a desi mardi gras. technicolour jealously protected from courier and airpacks and far too sterile frozen foods sections.

The Extinction of Durians

Anna Onni

The year is 2099. We are all waiting for that count-down to usher in the twenty-second century. It doesn't have the same ring as the twenty-first. We got the funny feeling that the calendar itself has become weary of the constant tabulation of the number of rounds made around the sun and the regular accommodations made with the leap year.

This place is called Little Singapore. It is about the size of the Central Business District back in the original Singapore. Long before the ocean levels had permanently submerged whole stretches of coastlines and made its way upstream towards the inlands of all the continents in 2065, the government had publicly announced the plan to relocate the island to the Tibetan Plateau. This was a territory used as a bargaining chip. When Singapore was finally brought in as a neutral arbitrator to decide the Tibetan territorial disputes in 2043, China's hegemony of global trade and mass production had started to truly wane. Three Ministry of Foreign Affairs officials acted as independent members of a decision-making panel of the reformed United Nations' International Court of Justice which recognised nations and autonomous regions as subsidiary members with a carefully qualified position of representation.

By the time the waters rose, we were safely ensconced in our new home. The year 2055, the first centennial of our independence, was celebrated in Little Singapore.

Carting an entire country up to a rough patch of land on the Tibetan Plateau required some ingenuity, but since the flooding started mass evacuations and relocations had become rather routine. Still: deaths, many injuries, massive dislocation, but manageable crises. Not disasters as they used to be in the early 2000s. Little Singapore was encased in a heavily reinforced glass dome, safe from most harms. Especially the frequent acid rains blowing in from Chinese factories that were still illegally producing toxic products and by-products.

For Little Singapore, the barely self-replenishing birth rates and the exodus of exiles and elites over the decades were a severe strain on national identity. By the time 2085 rolled around, we had about a million and a half citizens and half a million permanent residents to worry about. We have fewer now. In any case, the Singaporean models of Special Economic Zones had guaranteed a partially replicated model of Jurong was connected to a massive agricultural complex called Avocado Heights. Global warming and its peculiar effect on harsh climates had given Tibetan farmers the strange opportunity of producing tonnes of avocados. The winters had turned milder and the summers less intense. Mexicans depended on Tibet for their supply of avocadoes, their own changed climate producing year after year of failed crops. Whereas in Tibet, avocado smoothies had replaced tea as the most commonly consumed drink. No other fruit flourished as well as these usually picky and easily bruised specimens.

Even though our dome kept us apart from the ideal conditions that enabled the growth of avocadoes, there was a severe shortage of names for the places in Little Singapore. It no longer made sense to give places names like "Sentosa Cove" or "Marina Bay Sands" or "Merlion Park". We were so far away from the sea in this landlocked plateau that we were perched atop. So Avocado Heights was our new name, and it gleamed with the shine of a well-earned status symbol.

There used to be this fad trend for avocados smeared on grilled bread. As a millennial delicacy alongside truffle oil and protein shakes, it was considered the healthy replacement of butter and the basic ingredient of guacamole. All over the now-defunct internet, there was widespread horror at how a vehicle filled with 40,000 pounds of the fruit burst into flames at Christmastime. Avocadoes played a pivotal role in the blatant culturally appropriative American-Mexican cuisine, leading to protests in 2025, revealing a major loophole in the liberal activist culture that erupted with social media and hashtags. #guacamole allowed them to make their voices heard both locally and internationally. Rapidly breaking the algorithm shackles that #representation was limited to, #avocado was the gateway to being heard.

From hipster food to the symbol of the resistance, avocadoes were booming out of the surrounding territories around us. We even had a sizeable and almost self-sustaining crop inside our own Avocado Heights. Tibet was mass producing the one-time delicacy as the answer to the problem of a healthy diet. Since starch was out and veg was in, the least offensive of the offerings of roughage were offered as the new linings for concerned stomachs. In fact, the entire complex was successful at solving the world's problems. Green energy was finally mastered after decades of trying. It was just as well: humans had polished off all kinds of fossil fuel. Most of our green energy comes from the treacherous natural disasters that beat against the surface of the glass dome and the area around it.

Of all the great accomplishments of the soon-to-end 21st century, what all the great minds couldn't solve was the end of the durian species.

Durio zibethinus did not survive global warming. Or rather, it took ten years too long to mature into a fruiting tree, and the scientists had found a way of making polymers which could reliably produce the texture and taste of expensive durians. The industry slowly waned to a few shoddy outposts across Malaysia and Thailand, before a destructive heat wave in 2078 ravaged the remaining crop. After decades of intense selection and cross-fertilisation and genetic engineering – they wilted. Any other attempts in restoring the species found that the sea had crept into the water table and the plants were dying from the salinity. A few trees may have survived somewhere, but despite the tempting promise of mao shan wangs, X.O., and D24, no one had the patience to wait ten years to taste and see that the seed was bad. That the entire plot of fertile soil had been wasted on bad durians.

I ate my last seed in 2083. It was stale, dry, and was a brilliant shade of yellow which belied the powdery blandness that it tasted of. The good durians, even the middling durians, were more expensive than truffles were in the nineteenth century. They were more expensive than crack cocaine at the end of the twentieth century. The routes for drug trafficking were easily converted into durian trafficking. Where thousands upon thousands of the spiky fruit had once been driven easily through the borders they were now hoarded in fridges and frozen in boxes.

Meanwhile, all the possible combinations of durian sauces, durian cakes, durian jellies, durian marzipan, durian ice-creams, and durian soft drinks had been launched for cheap in the stores and supermarkets. They flooded the system with advertisements and vintage footage of the 1964 movie The 7th Dawn, based off the 1960 novel *The Durian Tree* by Michael Keon. This tropical image of rainforests and guerrilla insurgents jarred against the vivid oozing yellow of durian sauces expelled from guns and oozing out of wounds. They were an appetising egg-yolk colour in these advertisements, and tasted a little like an artificial banana sauce in real life.

These plastic durian polymers failed to give me the same pleasure I once had with the real fruit. To everyone else, I am a silly old woman who thinks too much of the past. The polymers were like those placebo pills that doctors used to give to people suffering from mental illnesses in the 2040s. Terrified of a looming diagnosis epidemic and a misuse of psychiatric drugs they cut access to mood stabilisers, uppers, and downers. Just like the doctors' silly pills these fake flavours do nothing for me. I miss the fresh air, and I want to go back to my little island home that is now bubbling under the risen oceans.

I have a little collection of saplings at my window. I was told that they were grown from durian seeds by a friend who sold them to me. I did not trust him, but I loved these little plants. They grew slowly, and I was desperately afraid that they would die.

Since moving into the glass dome, residents were not allowed to keep any indoor plants. We have artificial trees lining the streets. All green foliage was kept inside Avocado Heights. Anyone entering or exiting the compound was required to have a green pass and had to go through extensive checks before being led into a decontaminating room. I was too old to be considered for a green pass, which was mainly to make sure that children and young adults could get occasionally acclimatised to pollen and other allergens and microorganisms in the plants. Since the mosquitoes and cockroaches were still very much alive and happy outside our dome and had sneaked into Avocado Heights, there was a constant need to make sure that as few of the pests crawled into the domestic dwellings in the dome. Since fumigation would merely fog up and stay within the dome, the only alternative was to guard each entry and exit with the severity of a nuclear facility.

But I miss the green spaces, the sense of everything living and breathing alongside me. In this residential tower I only hear the complaints and smell the farts of everyone else. I am sick of avocado smoothies all the time because nothing else is cheap enough or soft enough for my poor gums and throat.

The only thing I enjoy now are the tiny durian trees. My little saplings are my secret, and I keep them carefully tucked away in the dark corner in my closet every time there is a room inspection. On other days, I hide them in a cluster of artificial plants. They sneak a fair amount of sunlight from their shaded spot and I always made make to have taller artificial plants at hand to surround them as they grow larger.

Whenever I have a free moment, which is a lot of the time, I sit in my living room surrounded by all my plants. This habit makes all my neighbours think that I am downright raving mad. No one sits in one place like this anymore. There was no point in fingering fake plants. It is like wanting a real tiger as your pet while you stroked a stuffed toy. Plants were deadly. They were carriers of contagions, dangerous stuff. Plants were an alien species to the most of the residents except the old-timers like me.

There are only a handful of us in this tower and none of us likes each other. I'm the slut who is still talking about feminism decades after it has become irrelevant. Edward is the rich man who literally rubs all his new gadgets in our faces because he wants us to see the details with our fading vision. Joanna is the woman who tries and fails to make avocado baked goods. While we are no longer on speaking terms, she still sends baskets of avocado muffins and guacamole cakes that were baked in her failing and outdated oven. I have a feeling that she has poisoned them.

The other old folks are happily living with their families, and most still have their spouses with them. We have nothing in common to talk about.

None of them know how to play mah jong.

The great dome itself feels like the confining ceiling of one of those bygone cathedrals. We wanted to be saved from the rising tides, and we were. In a way. I grew up thinking that I would be able to spend my old age eating durians for dessert and licking the flesh off my fingers. Now whenever I mumble about durians the social worker, poor sweet young thing, thinks I want some durian mush from a factory and gives me a boxful of chemically produced sweets at her next visit.

I have to keep my little durian trees a secret from her. One day they won't be so little anymore. They are currently being crowded out and hidden by some big fake hedges. Soon I'll have to buy a small forest of bamboo and Christmas pines to block them entirely from view. I'll die before they ever produce any fruit, which means they will probably kill off my darlings when they come to clean up my rooms. Perhaps I'll make friends with one of the young workers at Avocado Heights. They live in greenery every work day. They'll understand. Perhaps they even managed to save some durian trees from extinction and are trying to breed a new line of better tasting durians again. Then the king of fruits will rule again and we can eat something other than these stupid avocadoes.

Dr M. Selvaraj's Mock Meat Deli

What to Write About in Cold Storage, Circa 2000 AD

Alvin Pang

Half-asleep, and holding the red earth of here and now
close at hand, it is easier, I suppose, to walk past the battlefield
that is real grass, into the cool shade of track lighting, reconditioned
air hinting at just the right scent of harvest time, bouquet of peaches,
fresh lime with an aftertaste of new apples. Reminds you of autumn,
if you've ever known such a thing as leaves dying into colour
and fruit bursting their seams like dresses shrunken from the wash,
like prisoners given amnesty for an hour choosing art over hunger.
The idea of choice, need turned into gold. Sail past the verdant aisles
of kai lan, dou miao, basil, asparagus, beet. Ponder the introversion
of mushrooms, the luscious enticement of tomatoes, firm grip
and fullness of ripe flesh. Pick a pasta, any pasta, their cryptic
labels slip your tongue as easily as Latin, finger the cheeses, how
any civilisation could think of eating mouldy curds
and at these prices. Finish off at the billboard:
lost pet, spare kittens, maid seeks expat family, garage sale,
english tuition, native speaker, results guaranteed.

And you tell me there's nothing to write about, that life
has handed you a blank sheet and you're just waiting in line
to pay up and get out. You could even be right. Maybe this is
all there is: moving on, moving up, a queue line
of souls waiting for checkout and proceeding to wherever.
The cash register bleats its numbers into view, there's
the sudden sharp smell of fresh money changing hands, plastic
bags rustling frantically to be on their way.
Or this could be nothing at all, backdrop against which
you ought to scrawl a life less ordinary, dress down,
get your hands dirty in the real stuff. Bloody your fists
against the hard edges of the world. Think deep thoughts.
Change the world. Get a life. Well,
your car's parked outside, here's the shopping the keys,
when you're done come upstairs – dinner's at seven.

Self-Portrait as Sheng Siong Outlet

Anurak Saelaow

Failing to cohere within the glass, I pause
in this torrential light. Beyond the sloping form
of fridges and aisles, something akin to life
emerges. A fount of bargains – bedecked and kind,
sanitary and becoming. An id congeals itself
from the tangle of a receipt, suddenly double

in the scratchy, convoluted loop of those double
speakers placed overhead. Let's pause
the announcements, briefly, to gather the self –
in this open bin is fruit of all manner and form.
From old world and new, arrayed in a kind
of mocking cornucopia. "*But it is life*

englobed," concludes the master, as if life
itself were the purpose of it, and not this double-
bind of comfort or meaning: a cry for kind
material hands to reach down and cradle us. Or pause,
briefly, this sudden fever, nebulous in form,
that gnaws away at any sense of self.

It is, after all, the lingering ghost of self
that activates these glassy doors. A measure of life
whispered through the vents, a shimmery form
strolling through rows to meet its earthly double.
Unspool the security footage. Press pause
at the right moment and the dust forms a kind

of constellation. It is, perhaps, unkind
to reveal that wavering and obscure self
that swims always inward between the pause
of the comma and the comma. Or to unearth life

from these lines, this gap of air, the double-
spaced shelves crossing this chamber's form.

So: Brush your hair. Unfold that cobalt uniform
and step into the buzz. Half of mankind
throngs into the breach between these double
doors. In this rush you must gird yourself
or backspin into a spectral mode of life.
Apples, bruised or whole, roll without pause

into the plastic bag's yielding form. This self,
scattered as it is, aligns into a kind of life.
I spot my glassy double and fail to pause.

superstar cereals

Anna Onni

bought at the one-dollar-only store
have a special toy inside for poor kids
melted plastic shapes make contact
with cardboard grains slightly thicker
than the boxes they half-filled
the rest is air that chokes and stales
even the tiny marshmallow bits
which could be more plastic
that fell off the skin tattoos of pop
tarts and stars that grinned inanely
that brothers connived to paste on
each other giggling about bad mistakes
made in thailand when by u.s. marines
and sisters swallowed silently singing
the advertisements for great gifts
and christmas carols for santa
but when everyone else is asleep
that is when the curious creature
obediently eating the food dry
without milk creeps to the waste
bin and drags out the real prize
of the box that she snips and cuts
and nips and tucks until it becomes
the stargazer's telescope that sees
astronomical scales of pinprick lights
even now at six and going seven
even after school rips out her cereal box
and forces her to consume milk
to gain weight the cartons and straws
don't tantalise her heart like the dollar
vending machines of parental scrimping
that bought her nutrients to grow up
and were snatched away by the lack
of gold stars on papers and ticks in boxes

Ode to Exotic Vegetables

Kucinta Setia

Fetch, chop and feast a batch of matching kohlrabies
thy windy smooch of tunnel's summer rain
that flourish hand in hand with air of glories
that moistens the soil of windmill's Rahael-like plain
and sprouts to azures are roots of rosemary
or those twittering are oozing carbohydrates
hissing in like flying saucers to my kitchenry
cracking like gold bars out of volcanoes, romas or chicory
like a sage slicing, sitting on a plain of brakes
life is hot, ringing on a windmill's cherry.

Brightness is gushing on grace of fantasy
the old banana shofar trumpets David's triumph
a dill is tilted in an angle towards the city
rhubarbs, rosy barks when crushed underneath drum
as the jobless and careless, the busy and fury—
memories of ribena days gushing up to those needy
an auid lang syne treat for friends and families
savour soupy, tasty, stalky
spas of sparse sanctity
nostalgic resonance of heaven sink to edible lilies.

That enters Eden are feasts of healthy sanctuaries
turns our red to green, downpour to drizzles
the gushing feeling in tummies
melting meaty minerals into animated Arnold muscles
my veggies in my country, reign to be ticked
equatorial and imperial, exotic and erotic
crunching caixin is thy power for spinach
fresh seeking duties of organ-playing on oregano picked
eminent and exotic, elaborate and elastic
thinking, dietary is more than longevity for longish.

Meditation over a Tecnogas Cooker

Leong Liew Geok

No – it's not the stove's anniversary:
From necessity I meditate
As latticed squares of squid simmer
With translucent onions in tomato sauce;
I conjure essay possibilities
For morning's promised distribution,
Turning Lawrence Forster Conrad Golding
Into student stuffing.

The steamy sources of inspiration,
Heat of blue gas, sharp smell of ketchup
In my fly-free, white-tiled kitchen
Are far from the Marabar Caves;
Then let temporal and transcendent combine
In the gut and heart of this house
Where each day, hunger is satiated
When we linger over bones,
Sitting ritual through.

The white squid's done.
Piggy is *passé*, Simon is gone.
Marlowe and Kurtz I'll serve with dessert;
Mosque and Temple can withdraw to wait
The time when they *should* be my nightcap –
Since dinner is almost ready –
Just minced meat and cabbage left
To cook with Lawrence Gertrude Miriam Paul.

The Poppadum Man

Ng Yi-Sheng

Once upon a time, there was an old woman who lived in a village. She decided to make a poppadum man. She mixed together chickpea flour and pepper and cumin and water, and cut it into the shape of a little sahib, with lentils for his eyes, a garlic clove for his mouth, and tiny little nuggets of aloo for the buttons of his waistcoat. Then she fried him in a pot of hot oil.

However, as his edges began to curl and his body grew crispy, the poppadum man leapt up out of the pot and ran out of the hut. The old woman chased after him, but the poppadum man shouted back, “Run, run, as fast as you can! You can’t catch me, I’m the poppadum man!”

Past the market he ran, and into the village square, where he met a cow. “Moo, I want to eat you!” said the cow, who galloped after him. But the poppadum man ran even faster, chanting, “Run, run, as fast as you can! You can’t catch me, I’m the poppadum man!”

A little further on, he ran into a temple and met a priest, performing a puja with his lamp and his bell. “Namaste, I want to eat you!” said the priest. But the poppadum man hopped over the heads of the worshippers, chanting, “Run, run, as fast as you can! You can’t catch me, I’m the poppadum man!”

Down the road, he ran into a railway station and met a group of European backpackers, grubby and rasta-haired and smelling of hash. “Grüß dich, we want to eat you!” said the backpackers. But the poppadum man sprinted at breakneck speed, even faster than the speeding train, chanting, “Run, run, as fast as you can! You can’t catch me, I’m the poppadum man!”

In the blink of an eye, he ran into a city and met a horde of technopreneurs. “Howdy, we want to eat you!” said the technopreneurs. But the poppadum man dodged their grasping paws, eluded their hungry efforts to crack his recipe and franchise him as a nouveau health food in Silicon Valley and Shanghai.

Finally, the poppadum man reached the sea. “Oh no!” he cried. But then, out of the waters rose Annalakshmi, the goddess of sustenance, seated on a lotus blossom and garlanded with jasmine.

"Little poppadum man, why do you ignore your destiny?" she chided him. "Remember, we all bound together in samsara, the eternal cycle of birth and death."

"How true," thought the poppadum man, and he sat down and started to meditate.

And as he sat there on the sand, with his crispy little legs folded into themselves, the technopreneurs, the backpackers, the priest, the cow, and last of all the little old lady, descended upon him. And as he reached the utmost state of enlightenment and bliss, they broke him apart, dipping his hands and feet and face into saucers of mint and yoghurt and chutney, then down into their hungry gullets.

"All is one," he said. And that was the end of the poppadum man.

The Apples

Cyril Wong

The apples wait in a bowl, so pick one; the apples tug at the hem of my hunger – the love of apples; they appear in a poem about a bowl of apples; they are as serene as monks; apples cannot know the colour of the bowl they are in; apples in a poem are not edible; neither is the bowl; the apples fight for my attention; in fact, this happens very slowly; the apples revel in their nudity and know nothing about sin; they genuinely believe they are the original fruit; the apples sometimes wish they were more than themselves; they have heard of apples larger than themselves; apples deny any relationship to pears; the apples wonder if it is true, that green apples exist; the apples riot in the dark, but cannot win; still, they try; the apples provide a reminder that time is never still; the apples fear what awaits them after they have been eaten; these apples would like to be reborn with legs; the apples are too restless to meditate; the apples were communist, but soon they converted to capitalism; they knock each other off the top of the bowl – the politics of apples; the apples curse quietly when one of them is chosen; and dream of orchards, the generosity of rain and sunlight; they remember suspension, gravity, then falling – ...apples mourn when none of them is chosen; the apples concede to my teeth, filling my mouth with their insides; unlike us, preferring time to hurry; the apples at the bottom admire those apples at the top; the apples wait to steal your life and turn it into an apple; unable to think beyond the bowl's bright rim, the open window; the apples are still waiting.

The Fried Chicken

Jennifer Anne Champion

The Fried Chicken was first discovered shortly after the extinction of the Fried Dodo bird.

The Fried Chicken can reach a ground speed of about 15 km/hr and in flight it could reach up to 25 km/hr or even more, depending on who's throwing it.

The Fried Chicken has survived because of its diversity and its ability to adapt. You can find it in a variety of habitats, for example, a lush, green salad. Or in groups of five or more, as they do in Buffalo. Occasionally, it's even hiding in the tundra of your refrigerator, but not for long.

The Fried Chicken is both solitary and gregarious.

The Fried Chicken should not be confused with the chicken nugget.

Chicken nugget is dead chicken.
The Fried Chicken is alive, with flavour.

Catching The Fried Chicken requires cunning, quick thinking, and crossing the road as good Fried Chicken invariably lives on the other side of your house.

Many purveyors of The Fried Chicken advertise authenticity and tasteful refinement such as to be found in Kentucky.

However, it is useful to note that one cannot be certain one has encountered The Fried Chicken if it does not have a head.

Real Fried Chicken has a head.

And a face.

But the best Fried Chicken, might even have a name.

Now, not many people know this but The Fried Chicken is an endangered speci. And there have been horrific experiments when it comes to its procreation.

Some experiments have included:

stuffing mushroom
inside bacon
inside The Fried Chicken.

But many experts believe that the only thing that should be stuffed in The Fried Chicken is The Fried Chicken.

And naysayers should just take that chicken and stuff it in their mouths.

12 True and Little-known Facts About Swee Choon Tim Sum

Valen Lim

1. At 25/7, Swee Choon has the longest opening hours of any dim sum place in Singapore.
2. One in every 14,592 *char siew paus* contains a "*Golden Angbao*", which permits five lucky patrons to enter the mysterious chamber known as "the Kitchen". It is unknown what happens inside, but lucky patrons have never been seen again.
3. The name, "Swee Choon", actually has another meaning: "Choon" means "*Spring*" in Chinese, and "Swee" means "Swee" in Singlish.
4. No-one knows when Swee Choon first opened. There are no records.
5. If you want your steamed tau sar paus fried, all staff are permitted to call you out loudly on your bad taste while also filming the event. The video is then forwarded to the "*Dim Sum Dollies*", a clandestine council set up to oversee that all dim sum is eaten properly and with respect. It is unknown what they do with the videos.
6. The plates are actually edible.
7. Swee Choon first became popular as a supper destination due to a viral marketing campaign during the early 2000s, which featured the slogan "*first you Jiak Kim, then you Jiak Dim Sum*".
8. Swee Choon (SCP-1965) is also classified as a Euclid-class anomaly. SCP-1965 is home to a temporal anomaly whereby any customer, regardless of the time of visit, will leave satiated at 2.02am. Attempts to leave the premises prior to this timing result in [DATA EXPUNGED].
9. In Season 2, Episode 4 of *The X Files*, Swee Choon appears in the back ground for 3 seconds.
10. There is a provision in the Constitution which provides for the continued running of Swee Choon for at least the next half-century.
11. Once every fortnight, Swee Choon hosts a fight club. Unfortunately, having written this piece, I have become barred from said club.
12. During the Spring Equinox, the first ray of sunlight shines perfectly through the doors and onto the cashier. Some say that if you manage to witness this phenomenon, you'll be blessed with good food for the whole year.

Unreadable Patterns Rising from the Insistence of Flow

Anurak Saelaow

Seated, we wait for carts to swivel by
and deliver their bounties of starch —
translucent or firm, girded in bamboo,

each morsel named and announced
by anonymous bearers. The carpet,
vaguely maroon, boasts a nebulous

tessellated design, announcing itself
ad nauseum in the general din.
Having done away with menus,

we trust in the providence of these
apron-clad ladies to summon that
which is heaved onto our plates —

stochastic elements of sesame
or tart, pudding and chicken-claw.
Filling ourselves up in acts

of unguided consumption.
I watch Sam split a bun
with his fingers: his nails

puncture crust like eggshell,
revealing its gift of steam,
the sudden redness of flesh.

A Phenomenological Cookbook

Daryl Lim Wei Jie

Bring some water to a boil. Peel the tomatoes, or don't.
That merino sweater is lovely, but not ideal for today's exertions.
Capture the setting sun in your saucepan, and panic
at your idle hurtling towards the grave. Make love
while waiting for the dough to rise. Consider how the fork
is really an extension of yourself. Bend the tines
to know the fork for the first time. Beat the eggs
with a fork you haven't ruined. Take a nap
and wake up with a whole new mood. The olive oil
should now disclose a tang of anxiety. If you must light up,
please look into the distance for the whole duration.
Note how cigarette smoke is distinct
from the scent of burning. When calling for pizza,
be authentic to your need. Demand things not on the menu.
Better to starve than to eat what everyone else is eating.

the grammar of a dinner

Arthur Yap

let's have chicken for dinner.

somewhere else, someone else utters:
let's have john for dinner.
we are alarmed by the latter
but a dinner, too, has its own grammar
& we are assured by grammarians
both utterances are in order.

john, + animate, + human,
couldn't be passed off as repast.
chicken is + animate, – human,
& can end up in any oven.
if we combine the items of grammar
the way things in cooking are,
we would then have:
let's have chicken for john for dinner,
let's have chicken for dinner for john,
let's have for john chicken for dinner,
let's have for dinner for john chicken;
but probably not:
let's have john for chicken for dinner,
let's have for dinner john for chicken.

john is a noun holding knife & fork.
chicken collocates with the verb eat.
grammarians favour such words
as delicious & john eats happily,
but in a gastronomic dinner
taxonomic john isn't to eat deliciously.

Bad Pizza in Late Capitalism: Ad Copy

David Wong Hsien Ming

The product,

drawn and quartered across flour-tipped aluminium
by guinea pigs with the might of genetically-modified phantom hunger
that guests are invited to trigger with the sound of a camera-click,

is

an open concept from a kitchen famous for eschewing the constraints of modern Singapore on a metaphorical level,
literally priming the population for the late 21st Century
with its sociological approach to creativity.

The establishment

sources produce entirely from the Svalbard Global Seed Vault,
introducing Nordic essentialism to the local imagination.
A revolution, quiet as the invention of air-conditioning.

Bad Pizza in Late Capitalism: Critic's Tweet

David Wong Hsien Ming

No doubt
given the micromanaged dough,
the sad look on the face of the buffalo mozzarella
– I am tasting a corporation's latex-covered index.

The air inside the crust: better than air outside it
the way inside is better than outside
in our climate; a choosing of sterility
over discomfort.

I did not take a picture;
here is my mother's.

Avocadean Business Strategies

Ho Kin Yunn

I paint my walls with ethograms of fruits
the berries are grouped together, as they are just before the scythe
point to which my art is held: it imitates horticultural life
The citruses keep to one category
ranked by misunderstood acidity; regardless, they strive to outsour one another
You'd think the stone fruits exhibit greater solidarity
Not necessarily. I've gathered them on my wall's dampest tuft
as if the juice of their being doesn't erode their cores fast enough

but the avocado

the avocado promises much in an age
where truth ripens or rots based on climate, depending
and Dave had an aneurysm while eating one; he died later, sleeping
people mourned, while many others reasoned
there are plenty of Daves in this world
but not enough non-fenced corporations
serving quality avocado toast
The avocado looks at a peach and goes
weren't we priced equally before?
Now every dish is unequivocally blessed by its presence
So it demands to be grouped with everything
as I artlessly do the wielder its bidding
planting ground beef on my patio wall
While Dave peers over the fence
in indignation, yet pining
for more.

mock meat

Ng Yi-Sheng

I am frightened by his mouth,
which makes the body out of bread,

milk from a grain of rice,
butter from cottonseed,
cream from almonds.

He pauses to swallow the wine.
Beneath the silver platter,
an eye of yolk
gleams at me from a nest of tofu.

He summons a roosters breast
from an ear of wheat; the hind of a pig
from a mound of garbanzo; a flurry
of white doves
from a rock of black fungus.
He wipes his chin.

From soy and onions: the loins of a calf, the liver of an ox.
Every forkful,
blessed with a soul
before passing his lips.

I am frightened of his mouth.
What creature are you, I whisper,
that drinks no blood but of your own creation?

He grins,
leans across the table,
and cracks open my breast like an eggshell.

And like a surgeon,
plucks out a perfect
apple
blossom.

Scramble

Margaret Louise Devadason

L. 'lamina' (metal plate) > 'lamella' (small metal plate) > Fr. '(la) lemelle' (omelette) > '(l')alemelle) > '(l')amelette' > '(l')omelette' (cf. L. 'ovum', egg) > Am. E. 'omelet'

O metal
plate, laminate,
O thin and lovely
knife; O fine-cooked
egg, determiner
of present dreams,
your determination
re-parsed; O re-parcelled
diminutive, O metathetic
mirage, tell us what
you know of history.
Of the irregular ovum;
its antecedent. Of its
regularisation.
Of the blade
as it falls.

The Satay Monologues

Meiko Ko

One day, the Satay Man says, "The future of this country lies in its sauce." That, in order to brew the final sauce of surrender — one that will answer all questions of the future, correct any previous errors and erratic migratory genes – it is vital that we write down, in the red handbook of the Hawker's Manifesto – so as to claim, this perfect right, to the original hue of the satay sauce, rich and thick, on the whites of a styrofoam bowl, exquisitely spiced and golden with divine sweetness – these following words:

"Drive north, where there is still land for peanuts. At the border to Malaysia, stop and ponder the sunder made of water from the straits, snaking into the South China Sea. Where the yellow tints from the brilliant sun skip upon waves, now ebbing below the span of the causeway. From now on this land is Malaysia, with the soft brown earth of Johor quietly bearing your steps. Look up and see afar, in this new town, installed with the latest condominiums and technology, buildings rise forth. Admire their sincerity to the sky, Malayan and broad and unforgiving, where birds speed past into the fortresses of jungles, and hills climb the earth with trees. Watch for an ancient banyan at a T-junction, turn right there and drive up a hill. At the top, there's a small peanut field. Park. See a fence. Behind it, rooted in soil, is the most perfect bunch of peanuts, located in a small plot. Walk alongside and count to the twentieth column, proceed into the dirt path and seek the fifteenth peanut shrub. The leaves will be yellow. Finger for a pod and open it, find in the inner shells veins browned, the skins of seeds pink and papery. With both hands, dig and with light tugs, pull out the shrub. Shake away extra soil and put it in a bag, know that this dialogue of peanuts, severed from its fundamental earth, is the secret taste responsible for the eventual satay sauce. Drive back to the causeway. Now dusk hangs like a pale curtain and the city lights are up. Should a man be dazzled by the glittering lights ahead, tell him that he's driving into the future, where he has come from and shall return, tell him further to observe his hands, see what they are doing in the present, now, while there's still daylight. Never doubt a path. Some consequences are too heavy to bear. At the Eunos exit, drive on the local roads south and see the forgotten lanes, lonely and dark. Nearby are the uncharted corners of void decks and forlorn voices of crickets. Ahead is a hawker centre, bright, a fortress of movable feasts in a swarm of smoke, enter it and weave your way through its usual stalls and tables till you find the Satay Man. There he is. Standing with his rattan fan, his hand maneuvering the threaded meat above a charcoal grill. Speak to him, say hello uncle, I've come to pass you this bag of peanuts and this little red book, the Hawker's Manifesto, written to decide the verbs and tastes of our future tongue: *I am the Satay Man, I am who I am, now I am old, the future of my sauce for this country will die in my hands, my recipe secret and going with me to the grave.* He'll know what to do with the items, while he busies himself with the assam and galangal and lemongrass. Some time later, he'll bring to your table the bowl of sauce, creamy and conclusive, a film of oil hovering like a layer of red seduction, and setting it down, he shall say, "Now enjoy, this culture of food, while it lasts, in my sauce are peanuts that have traveled far, every day I wait for them, and waiting is one of the ingredients I use in my bowl of satay sauce."

A few months later, at the same Hawker Centre:

"Hello, I'm from China, and I'm taking over the Satay Man's Stall, somewhere in Geylang Serai. For you see, life in China is crushing me. Each day men without work sit on railings in the big city I was born, smoking cigarettes and loitering, hands in pockets and thinking idle thoughts, there are not enough jobs. But I am refusing to die. I'd heard about the Chinese of Southeast Asia, making fortunes with peanuts in their pockets, carrying lanterns for the eighth moon like ourselves, but when I got here I could not understand their staccato tongues and imported vocabularies, tell me left and I'd turned right, tell me lower the heat but I fired it up, bring me the assam and I thought it dung. But I am taking over the Satay Man's Stall, because no one here wants to carry on. Now we don't need the *assam*, I say, or the *gula melaka*, or the chili and tumeric, these are ingredients Arabic to me, I'll season the meat with a different concoction, replace them with dried lotus herbs in the skewers. The fire is intense, lean and sharp and escaping wild through the grills, and the basting oil is dripping. From the fridge I take out the rice squares, which I pre-ordered from a *ketupat* dealer, and the onions, which I can quarter with no worries, and arranging these all on a plate, with the satay sticks spreading like a peacock's tail, I present to you, this new breed of satay from my New Satay Stall. Hello, my name is Bingxu, and I'm from China. I hope you'll enjoy my satay of the future, and please, come again, I'll be around in hawker centre, Geylang Serai."

When the World Ends You Will Be Eating Hokkien Mee

Stephanie Chan

When the last panda dies from an overdose of Viagra in some zoo that he was sent to as a cub as a last-ditch-attempt-at-peace-type goodwill gift from China, you will be counting how many pieces of sotong the stallholder gave you.

Whentheoceansstartoverflowingandstartswallowingupsmallcoastalcities, the death toll will not even reach the 6pm news on the hawker centre TV.

When all the fish have gone extinct, and all the chickens have died of some flesh-eating version of bird flu that also managed to wipe out three developing countries in two months, it will be ok: there will always be enough prawns left in the sea.

When the tidal waves start flooding large coastal cities like Sydney, LA and Vancouver, there will still not be enough lard in your Hokkien mee.

When the earth starts to crack open and swallow up Jakarta and Tokyo, you might be intrigued by the noodles on your plate trembling ever-so-slightly from the tremors.

When buildings in Malaysia start to collapse from the tremors, believe that it was because they were poorly built anyway.

When a malaria epidemic hits Southeast Asia, remember to swallow your government-sponsored malaria vaccine after your meal and thank God you live in a functional country.

When the threat of nuclear war is imminent but probably won't make much of a difference at this point in history, keep believing that Hokkien mee noodles grow out of the ground on a farm somewhere in Kranji.

When the ocean starts to encroach a little bit on reclaimed land in Changi, Jurong Island, the CBD, just remember you were never promised that Singapore would be 'flood free'.

When the first child dies in a flooded neighbourhood on the ECP, be glad you live on the 20th floor.

When the first families are lost to a tsunami in Pasir Ris, you will be eating Hokkien mee.

When Resorts World disappears underwater, you will be eating Hokkien mee.

And it will be damn good Hokkien mee. So good you will want another, but you will never get another because the stall owner will be dead. And his wife will be dead. And his son, the only other person with the recipe in his head will not remember it because he fucked off years ago to open a gourmet dessert bar which only serves people who can say the words 'post-apocalyptic' with a straight face.

So go on, enjoy that plate of Hokkien mee: it will be the last plate of Hokkien mee you will ever taste, that will ever be tasted in the world, and be glad, be fucking glad, for when that tidal wave rears up to engulf this island and there is screaming everywhere and you finally look up and see the wall of water about to swallow the Old Airport Road hawker centre, the taste of prawn stock, lard and MSG will be the only thing left to hold on to.

Makan Again

Ann Ang

2020 will be remembered as a year of the interminable and the immeasurable. I say this as the circuit-breaker in Singapore is about to start, while no country has fully eradicated the novel coronavirus. The authorities say, for now, that lockdown will last for a month. In front of me is a plastic bento box of fried noodles, with a braised egg and prawn fritters – my luxury dinner ration – it is contained, itemised and disposable.

Though I've spent a week under quarantine in a government-designated hotel, food is not a concern. But it is an abiding, unrelenting obsession. "Three standard meals" a day is the only tangible contact I have with the world beyond my room door. When hotel staff leave the neatly packed bundle outside, they knock or ring the bell, and I shout "thank you" but never open the door. I must not forget – I might be infected; I may have Covid-19. Having returned home from the UK, where community transmission is at large, this is a possibility.

Living in a time of Covid-19 is about counting down the days, towards an end that seems to recede as we approach. There are some other numbers which are significant: the 14-day stay-home period if one has returned from abroad or the three-day wait for test results. You would want those few days to pass without further news – individuals who test positive are usually notified within twenty-four hours. Balanced against these finite figures are those that belie comprehension, such as the uncounted rows of coffins transported by military trucks in Italy, or 1500 deaths within twenty-four hours in the United States, or case 1052 in Singapore. Government spokespeople and news reports attempt to provide ways of breaking down these numbers, by classifying cases as locally transmitted or imported; by sharing the figures of those who have been discharged from hospital, or released from intensive care; or celebrating, however cautiously, a drop in the number of new cases reported daily.

Against the horror resulting from losing all sense of scale, and as the walls of our now-too-cosy apartments close in, there exists, unfailingly, the daily measure of the next meal. Not three meals for today, or tomorrow, but the onward, mundane, minutely-reviewed consideration of what we shall eat next and how to cook it, and procure the ingredients to do so. Those of us who can afford to stay and work from home, with a secure line of supply, are privileged. The hours to the next meal are interminable for those who do not know when they will next eat, or who are too ill to eat, or who are sick with fear over whether they will still be employed tomorrow. To quote a letter to America about its future (now its present), from Italian novelist Francesca Melandri, "First of all, you'll eat" and "You'll eat again." The time between one makan and the next, however, can be hard to measure, a period of gnawing, acidic waiting, punctuated by national addresses from the prime minister and more dire news from around the world.

The thrice-daily meal deliveries have become a conversation between the kitchen and me. I am told at length about the virus-busting properties of fresh-cut seasonal fruits: tart, ribbed guava slices, a golden kiwi, a blushing jambu and cubes of yellow watermelon studded with black seeds. They tell us we're already in Singapore, sending up fried carrot cake and nasi lemak, prawn noodles and chicken rice. It is all about balance: a breakfast of bircher muesli comes with a croissant; a dish of dry mee siam with a whole-grain roll. There is a grace note for each long afternoon, with petit-fours or dark chocolate mousse for tea. Between meals, I try to read the mind of the hotel's staff – what will they serve later? In the second week of self-isolation, will these deliveries continue to be as suggestively delightful as kueh? And as soon as there is the rustle of plastic from the corridor, I am at my door, feral and intent, all semblance of civilisation boiled down to the courtesy of waiting for that little knock, and for the porter to depart.

Occasionally there are dark moments when I wonder what will happen, when the lockdown begins. Will social order break down, and these meals stop coming? Down a dark well, this is a faint echo of makan, which I know as a word that must be used only in company. You makan already? Later where we going to makan? Another day we must makan. Makan is a plan, a place, and a memory, and here in self-isolation, makan is impossible, only corona-makan as a dwindling of the hours. The survivalist streak in me emerges strongly, honed from years of commemorating Total Defence Day in school with food and water rationing exercises. In the background, documentaries of the Japanese Occupation are screened, wailing with air-raid sirens. My peers and I eat our allotted sweet potatoes, reflecting not on our hunger but on what we would eat next, most likely a hot dinner at home.

On social media today, we chide each other today for panic-buying, but the fear of not having enough has deep roots. This is after all a country where scarcity is the default mindset despite immense wealth, and where we constantly emit predictive static to find out where the best eats are, and if there are enough parking lots at the mall we'll visit in an hour. Will social order break down under lockdown, I wonder? Already the restaurant industry is tottering and food businesses are making drastic changes to switch to an online model. Will we survive, without being able to eat at our beloved coffee shops? Perhaps tomorrow my meals will not be delivered, and I will have no choice but to take my valuables and the bread rolls I've stowed away, and emerge trotting quickly and quietly in the direction of my neighbourhood, past shuttered shops and the open boot of a car filled with abandoned toilet rolls. In these perilous times, no one will emerge from home, even for the best bak ku teh.

The contemplation of eating in a time of Covid-19 produces many strange thoughts. For circuit-breaking, good citizens will remain at home, contemplating the tropical, humid sky through their windows. The western press tends to identify Singapore as an authoritarian state, replete with surveillance and infringements on civil liberty. But they forget that Singaporeans, as the body politic, make up this nation. Many of us live in high-rise apartments and since time immemorial, have surveyed our neighbours and allowed ourselves to be watched in turn. Curtains are of no use when you raise your voice. Only this time, distance is ironically, a form of care. This is what freedom looks like during a plague, where the health of the herd is decided negatively, by individual decisions, and our individual lives are governed by the essential business of the next meal.

So first we'll eat. We'll weigh all the options about where to dapao from, or if we should turn chef ourselves by stewing jackfruit curry or fermenting our own tempeh. As the ancient Romans did, we'll plaster our walls with food images, by snapping endless photographs, sharing these on Instagram and having solitary dinners with our friends over facetime. Before we sleep, we'll look over these pictures, wondering about breakfast. If we are lucky, this too will pass, and going to the supermarket will no longer be a masked endeavour. Then we'll look out the window, invite a friend, open the door, and eat again.

ABOUT THE EDITORS AND WRITERS

AARON MANIAM's debut poetry collection, *Morning at Memory's Border*, was one of three books shortlisted for the Singapore Literature Prize in 2007. In 2003, he won the First Prize for English poetry in the National Arts Council's Golden Point Award. His second collection, *Second Persons*, was published in August 2018.

ALFIAN SA'AT is a Resident Playwright with Wild Rice. His published works include three collections of poetry, *One Fierce Hour*, *A History of Amnesia* and *The Invisible Manuscript*, a collection of short stories, *Corridor*, a collection of flash fiction, *Malay Sketches*, three collections of plays as well as the published play 'Cooling-Off Day'.

ALVIN PANG is a Singapore-based poet and editor. Featured in *The Oxford Companion to Modern Poetry in English* and *The Penguin Book of the Prose Poem*, he has been published internationally and translated into more than twenty languages. His latest book is *What Happened: Poems 1997-2017*.

AMANDA LEE KOE won the Singapore Literature Prize for her first short story collection, *Ministry of Moral Panic*. Her debut novel, *Delayed Rays of A Star*, was named a Best Book of 2019 by NPR.

DR ANITHA DEVI PILLAI is an applied linguist and teacher educator at National Institute of Education (NTU), where she teaches courses on writing pedagogy and writing skills. She has published books, academic papers, poems, short stories and articles in newspapers. Her next book is a full-length historical novel titled *Sembawang*.

ANN ANG is a published writer of poetry and fiction, and her work has appeared in *Quarterly Literary Review Singapore*, *Softblow*, *California Quarterly* and *The Jakarta Post*. She is also the author of *Bang My Car* (Math Paper Press, 2012), a Singlish-English collection of short stories. Ann is currently reading for a DPhil in English at the University of Oxford.

ANNA ONNI is an educator who illustrates and writes in her sketchbooks.

ANURAK SAELAOW has been published in *Cha: An Asian Literary Journal*, *Hayden's Ferry Review*, *Quarterly Literary Review Singapore*, *Cultural Weekly*, *The Kindling*, *Ceriph*, and elsewhere. He is the author of one chapbook, *Schema* (The Operating System, 2015), and holds a BA in Creative Writing and English from Columbia University.

ARIN ALYCIA FONG is a graduate student of Creative Writing at Nanyang Technological University. Her short fiction appears in *this is how you walk on the moon* and was longlisted for the First Pages Prize 2018 by Stockholm Writers' Festival. Her poetry and critical work are online at *Quarterly Literary Review Singapore*, *Jacket2*, and the *Anomaly* blog.

ARTHUR YAP (1943–2006), one of Singapore's most important poets, was awarded the Cultural Medallion for his contributions to literature in 1983. He was also a painter and a writer of short stories. *The Collected Poems of Arthur Yap* and *Noon at Five O'Clock: The Short Stories of Arthur Yap* are from NUS Press.

BOEY KIM CHENG was born in 1965 and emigrated from Singapore to Australia in 1997. He has published five books of poetry and a travel memoir. He taught writing at the University of Newcastle for thirteen years before joining the Nanyang Technological University in 2016.

BRANDON CHEW's works have been published in *Fish Eats Lion*, *Balik Kampung 4A*, *Ceriph*, and *Chubby Hubby*. He lives in San Francisco.

CATHERINE LIM is a writer of fiction and a commentator on social and political issues in Singapore. She has published numerous novels and short story anthologies. Before she became a writer, she was a teacher, linguistics lecturer and educational administrator. She has two children and lives in Singapore.

CYRIL WONG is a poet and fictionist in Singapore.

DAREN SHIAU, PBM, is a fiction writer, poet and editor. He was the National Arts Council's Young Artist of the Year in 2002, and has been described by *The Arts Magazine* as "among the most exciting" of the post-independence generation of Singapore writers. His works include a novel *Heartland* (1999), a poetry collection *Peninsular: Archipelagos and Other Islands* (2000) and a microfiction collection *Velouria* (2007).

DARYL LI is a writer of fiction and non-fiction based in Singapore. His work has been longlisted for the the *Australian Book Review* Calibre Essay Prize, placed second at the Golden Point Award competition, and appeared in *Quarterly Literary Review Singapore*. He works as an editor.

DARYL LIM WEI JIE is a poet and critic based in Singapore. He is particularly interested in the intersections between poetry and history. His first collection of poetry, A Book of Changes, was published by Math Paper Press in 2016 under the Ten Year Series imprint. His poems won him the Golden Point Award in English Poetry in 2015, awarded by the National Arts Council, Singapore.

DAVID WONG HSIEN MING's work has appeared in *Quarterly Literary Review Singapore* and *Mascara Literary Review*. His first collection, *For the End Comes Reaching*

(2015), is a meditation on the sense of loss that accompanies each having. davidwonghsienming.wordpress.com.

DESMOND KON ZHICHENG-MINGDÉ is a poet and fictionist, with fifteen authored books. A former journalist, he has edited over twenty titles. Among other accolades, Desmond is the recipient of the IBPA Benjamin Franklin Award, Independent Publisher Book Award, Poetry World Cup, Singapore Literature Prize, and three Living Now Book Awards.

EDDIE TAY is a poet, street photographer and literature professor based in Hong Kong. His most recent poetry and street photography collection is *Dreaming Cities* (2016). His recent book on creative writing, street photography and scholarship is *Anything You Can Get Away With: Creative Practices* (2018).

EDWIN THUMBOO is Emeritus Professor (1997) and Professorial Fellow, Department of English Language and Literature, National University of Singapore. His first collection of poems, *Rib of Earth*, was published in 1956, and his most recent volume of poems, *A Gathering of Themes*, appeared in 2019.

GOPAL BARATHAM (1935-2002) was a neurosurgeon and author. In 1982, his short story collection *Figments of Experience* won a Highly Commended award from the National Book Development Council of Singapore. His novel *A Candle or the Sun* (Serpent's Tail, 1991) was shortlisted for the Commonwealth Writers' Prize in 1992. Gopal was awarded the Southeast Asian Write Award in 1991. He passed away at the age of 66 from pneumonia.

HAMID ROSLAN's work may be found in *The Volta*, *Asymptote*, and *Quarterly Literary Review Singapore*, among others. *parsetreeforestfire* (Ethos Books, 2019) is his debut poetry collection.

HIDHIR RAZAK is an ardent believer of the power of storytelling and its unique ability to bring people and communities together. Hidhir is a reader, writer, and researcher by training. His writings have appeared in *The Middle Ground*, *Yahoo Singapore*, and *poetry.sg* while his creative works have appeared in numerous anthologies and collections in Singapore. He holds a Master of Arts degree from Nanyang Technological University where he specialised in English and Creative Writing.

HO KIN YUNN's work has appeared in anthologies such as *Twenty-Four Flavours*, *Anima Methodi*, *PLACES* (2018), *SingPoWriMo 2018*, as well as *Cha: An Asian Literary Journal*. Feel free to reach him at kinyunn@gmail.com.

IAIN LIM JUN RUI is a Singaporean poet and aspiring filmmaker currently reading Philosophy in Belgium. A two-time winner of the Love Poetry Competition and finalist in the National Poetry Competition 2017, his poetry is published in *OF*

ZOOS, *Voice & Verse Poetry Magazine*, *Rambutan Literary*, *Kitaab* and *Twin Cities*, among others. His first documentary short was a finalist at Singapore Heritage Short Film Competition 2017.

JACK XI (he/they) is a disabled queer poet. A member of the writing collective Stop at Bad End Rhymes (stylized /s@BER), they've been published in *Wyvern Lit*, *OF ZOOS*, *SingPoWriMo 2018*, and *Anima Methodi: The Poetics of Mirroring*.

JENNIFER ANNE CHAMPION is a writer, performance poet, educator and archivist. She co-founded poetry.sg, a digital archive for all things poetic and Singaporean. She co-organises Destination: Ink, Singapore's longest running open-mic night for live literary and musical experiments. She also authored two chapbooks: *A History of Clocks* (2015) and *Caterwaul* (2016), co-edited the *SingPoWriMo 2015* anthology and has been featured in several other anthologies and journals.

JINNY KOH is the author of *The Gods Will Hear Us Eventually* (Ethos Books, 2018). Her stories and essays have appeared or are forthcoming in *The Iowa Review*, *Pembroke Magazine*, *Carolina Quarterly* and *Kyoto Journal*, among others. She is a freelance editor and writer based in Singapore.

JOLLIN TAN writes about the body, memory, and art: in poetry, prose, and non-fiction. Her two poetry collections, *Bursting Seams* and *Derivative Faith*, are published by Math Paper Press. Jollin's work is curated in anthologies and places such as *Body Boundaries*, *SingPoWriMo The Anthology*, *Balik Kampung 3B: Some East, More West*, *Prairie Schooner* and Singapore Writers Festival.

JOSHUA IP is a poet, editor, and literary organiser. He has edited eight anthologies and written four poetry collections, most recently footnotes on falling (2018). He has won awards. He co-founded Sing Lit Station, a literary charity that runs community initiatives including SingPoWriMo, *poetry.sg* and several workshop groups. www.joshuaip.com.

KOH JEE LEONG is the author of *Steep Tea* (Carcanet, 2015), named a Best Book of the Year (2015) by *Financial Times* and a finalist by *Lambda Literary* in the USA. He has published three other books of poems, a volume of essays, and a collection of zuihitsu. His new book of poems is *Connor and Seal* (Sibling Rivalry, 2020).

KUCINTA SETIA (GAN YUNG CHYAN) had the first of his series of *ode to exotic fruits* poems published by *The Straits Times* on 26 July 1996. His first poetry collection is *Odes to Edibles* (Seaview Press, 1998). It was followed by *Asia.Peru Exports* (2005).

LEE TZU PHENG, ANNE has eight personal collections of poetry and has won numerous awards including the Singapore Cultural Medallion, the SEA Write Award, the Gabriela Mistral Award (Chile), the Montblanc-CFA Literary Award, and the Singapore National Book Development Council Award (Poetry) three times. Known for her clarity and understated humour, she is studied internationally, and has mentored many young writers.

LEONG LIEW GEOK taught in the Department of English Language and Literature, NUS, for twenty-one years. She has published two volumes of poetry, *Love is Not Enough* (1991) and *Women without Men* (2000). She edited *More than Half the Sky: Creative Writings by Thirty Singaporean Women* (1998; repr. 2009).

LYDIA KWA has published two books of poetry, *The Colours of Heroines* (Women's Press, 1994) and *sinuous* (Turnstone Press, 2013). Kwa's first novel *This Place Called Absence* (Turnstone, 2000) was nominated for several awards. Her next novel, *The Walking Boy*, was nominated for the Ethel Wilson Prize. *Pulse* (Key Porter Books, 2010), a novel set in Singapore and Toronto, was re-issued by Ethos Books in 2014. Her fourth novel, *Oracle Bone*, was published by Arsenal Pulp Press in 2017. A new version of *The Walking Boy* has just been released in Spring 2019 (Arsenal Pulp) as the second novel in the *chuanqi* 傳奇 trilogy.

MADELEINE LEE is an investment manager who also writes poetry. She has published 10 volumes of poetry, the latest being *regarding*, a volume of ekphrasic poems written during her year as Poet-in-Residence at National Gallery, Singapore.

MARGARET LOUISE DEVADASON is a Singaporean poet, currently pursuing a bachelor's degree at Nanyang Technological University. Shortlisted for the National Poetry Competition 2018, and winner of the poetry division of the 2018 NTU Creative Writing Competition, Margaret's work has appeared in anthologies including *SG Poems 2017-2018* and *Anima Methodi*.

MARGARET LEONG NÉE MCDANIELS (1921–2012), an American who moved from Missouri to Singapore in 1949, published two collections of poetry that took as their subject the natural and social worlds of Singapore and Malaya: *The Air Above the Tamarinds* (1957), and *Rivers to Senang* (1958). Leong also wrote children's verse, collected in *The Ice Ball Man* (2002).

MEIKO KO's works have been published by *The Literary Review*, *Columbia Journal*, *Epiphany*, *Vol. 1 Brooklyn*, *Litro*, *Five:2:One*, *Breadcrumbs*, *Crab Orchard Review*, *Scoundrel Time* (Pushcart Prize nomination), *failbetter* and elsewhere. She was long listed for the 2017 Berlin Writing Prize.

NABILAH SAID is a playwright, poet and arts writer. Her plays have been staged in Singapore and London, and her work has been published by Math Paper Press, Ethos Books and Nick Hern Books. Formerly with *The Straits Times*, Nabilah is currently the editor of regional arts website *ArtsEquator.com*.

NATALIE WANG writes about cats, ghosts, and womanhood. She is the author of

The Woman Who Turned into a Vending Machine (Math Paper Press, 2018), which is dedicated to the above subjects. www.nataliewang.me.

NG YI-SHENG is a multidisciplinary writer, cultural researcher and LGBT+ activist. His books include the short story collection *Lion City*, the best-selling non-fiction work *SQ21*, and three poetry collections: *last boy* (winner of Singapore Literature Prize 2008), *Loud Poems for a Very Obliging Audience*, and *A Book of Hims*.

PRASANTHI RAM is a Singaporean fiction writer. A PhD candidate for Creative Writing at Nanyang Technological University, she is working on a debut short story collection that examines the Tamil Brahmin community in Singapore. Her interests lie in South Asian anglophone literature, women's studies, as well as popular culture.

RODRIGO DELA PEÑA, JR. is the author of *Aria and Trumpet Flourish* (Math Paper Press, 2018). His poems have been published in *Quarterly Literary Review Singapore*, *Rattle*, *Hayden's Ferry Review*, *OF ZOOS*, and other journals and anthologies. Born in the Philippines, he has been based in Singapore since 2011.

RUTH TANG (they/them) is a playwright and poet. She lives, depending on the time of year, in New York City and Singapore.

SHIRLEY GEOK-LIN LIM's *Crossing the Peninsula* received the Commonwealth Poetry Prize. Awarded the Multiethnic Literatures of the United States Lifetime Achievement Award, she's published 10 poetry collections; three short story collections; three novels and *The Shirley Lim Collection*. Her memoir *Among the White Moon Faces* and anthology *The Forbidden Stitch* received American Book Awards.

SREEDHEVI IYER is the author of *Jungle Without Water* and *The Tiniest House of Time*. Her work has been shortlisted for a Pushcart Prize and the Penang Monthly Book Award, and appeared in *Hotel Amerika*, *Drunken Boat*, *The Writer's Chronicles*, Asian *American Literary Review*, *Ginosko Literary Journal* (US), *The Free Word Centre* (UK), *Two Thirds North* (Sweden), and *Cha: An Asian Literary Journal*, *Asia Literary Review* (HK).

STEPHANIE CHAN has won poetry slams in Singapore and the UK and runs a monthly poetry night in Singapore called Spoke & Bird. They are the author of a poetry collection called *Roadkill for Beginners* (Math Paper Press, 2019).

SUSHIRO (now OMOTÉ) is a sushi bar experience with the freshness served daily.

THEOPHILUS KWEK is a writer and researcher based in Singapore. The author of five volumes of poetry, he has been shortlisted twice for the Singapore Literature Prize, and serves as co-editor of *Oxford Poetry*. His essays, poems and translations have appeared in *The Guardian*, *Times Literary Supplement*, *The London Magazine*, and *Mekong Review*.

TOH HSIEN MIN has written four books of poetry, and won two blind wine-tasting competitions.

TONG JIA HAN, CHLOE, writes about food and family. She read World Literature at Warwick University and English at Nanyang Technological University, and is the co-author of a children's picture book, *The Phantom of Oxley Castle*.

TSE HAO GUANG's first full-length poetry collection, *Deeds of Light*, was shortlisted for the 2016 Singapore Literature Prize. He is a 2016 fellow of the University of Iowa's International Writing Program, and the 2018 National Writer-in-Residence at Nanyang Technological University. His new work-in-progress is tentatively called *I get buzzed seeing your hand's just left*.

VALEN LIM is a member of local literary collective /stop@BadEndRhymes ('/s@ber'). He can be found at uglystage.com.

WAHID AL MAMUN is a Singaporean of Bangladeshi origin currently studying at the University of Chicago with a view to majoring in Anthropology. His poem "my mother thinks i dream in bengali" received a honorable mention in the Sing Lit Station's inaugural Hawker Prize for Southeast Asian Poetry in 2018. His other works have appeared in *Quarterly Literary Review Singapore*, *the murmur house*, as well as numerous SingPoWriMo anthologies.

WONG MAY (b. Chungking, China) arrived in Singapore after World War II, leaving in 1966 to pursue an MFA at the University of Iowa. She married in 1973, and moved to Dublin with her family by 1987. Her poetry collections include *A Bad Girl's Book of Animals* (1969), *Reports* (1972), *Superstitions* (1978), and *Picasso's Tears* (2014).

WONG PHUI NAM began writing in the 1950s while a student in Singapore. He published his first volume of verse in 1967. Apart from original verse in English, he wrote "readings" of the Tang poets as he thought much of the splendour of their poetry was usually lost in scholarly translations. He continues writing today.

YONG SHU HOONG has authored six poetry collections, including *Frottage* (2005) and *The Viewing Party* (2013), which both won the Singapore Literature Prize, and *Right of the Soil* (2018). He is one of the four co-authors of *The Adopted: Stories from Angkor* (2015) and *Lost Bodies: Poems Between Portugal and Home* (2016).

PREVIOUSLY PUBLISHED WORKS

Aaron Maniam. "Pantun for a Drink Seller at Newton Circus". *Morning at Memory's Border* (firstfruits publications, 2005).

Alfian Sa'at. "8 Ways of Loving a Banana". *Love Gathers All*. Eds. Alvin Pang and Aaron Lee (Ethos Books, 2002).

---. "Fasting in Ramadan". *A History of Amnesia* (Ethos Books, 2001).

Alvin Pang. "Hunger". *City of Rain* (Ethos Books, 2003).

---. "What to Write About in Cold Storage, Circa 2000 AD". *City of Rain* (Ethos Books, 2003).

Amanda Lee Koe. "Randy's Rotisserie". *Quarterly Literary Review Singapore* (Vol. 11 No. 4, Oct 2012).

Arthur Yap. "the correctness of flavour". *The Collected Poems of Arthur Yap* (NUS Press, 2013).

---. "the grammar of a dinner". *down the line* (Heinemann Educational Books, 1980). Reprinted in *The Collected Poems of Arthur Yap* (NUS Press, 2013).

---. "on offal". *The Collected Poems of Arthur Yap* (NUS Press, 2013).

Boey Kim Cheng. "Soup". *Between Stations* (Giramondo, 2009). Reprinted in *Between Stations* (Epigram Books, 2017).

Brandon Chew. "Map of Seletar". *Balik Kampung 3A* (Math Paper Press, 2016).

Catherine Lim. "Durian". *Or Else, The Lightning God & Other Stories* (Heinemann Educational Books, 1980).

Cyril Wong. "The Apples". *Straw, Sticks, Brick* (Math Paper Press, 2012).

Daren Shiau. "Kentang". *Peninsular: Archipelagos and Other Islands* (Ethos Books, 2000).

Daryl Lim Wei Jie. "A Phenomenological Cookbook". *Quarterly Literary Review Singapore* (Vol. 16 No. 3, Jul 2017).

Eddie Tay. "A Lover's Soliloquy". *A Lover's Soliloquy* (Ethos Books, 2005).

Edwin Thumboo. "The Sneeze". *Gods Can Die* (Heinemann Educational Books, 1977).

Gopal Baratham. "The Wafer". *Figments of Experience* (Times Books International 1981). Reprinted in *Collected Short Stories Gopal Baratham* (Marshall Cavendish, 2014).

Hamid Roslan. "Besok sunrise egg still put". *parsetreeforestfire* (Ethos Books, 2019).

Hidhir Razak. "Nenek Taught Me To". *SingPoWriMo 2017: The Anthology*. Eds. Stephanie Chan, Ruth Tang and Daryl Qilin Yam (Math Paper Press, 2017).

Jennifer Anne Champion. "The Fried Chicken". *A History of Clocks.* (Red Wheelbarrow Books, 2015).

Jollin Tan. "Outpouring". *Derivative Faith* (Math Paper Press, 2013).

Joshua Ip. "dance of the tea eggs". *footnotes on falling* (Math Paper Press, 2018).

---. "first date at jumbo seafood". *making love with scrabble tiles* (Math Paper Press, 2013).

---. "soft-boiled". *sonnets from the singlish* (Math Paper Press, 2012).

Koh Jee Leong. ''A Lover's Recourse". *Seven Studies for a Self Portrait* (Bench Press, 2011).

---. "Hungry Ghosts". *Equal to the Earth* (Bench Press, 2009).

---. "Useless". *Steep Tea* (Carcanet Press, 2015).

Kucinta Setia (Gan Yung Chyan). "Ode to Exotic Vegetables". *Odes to Edibles: an anthology of Singapore dialect poems* (Seaview Press, 1998).

Lee Tzu Pheng, Anne. "Neanderthal Bone Flute: A Discovery". Lambada by Galilee and Other Surprises (Times Books International, 1997). Reprinted in Soul's Festival (Landmark Books, 2014).

Leong Liew Geok. "A Wet Market in Singapore". *Women Without Men* (Times Books International, 2000).

---. "Meditation Over a Tecnogas Cooker". *Love is Not Enough* (Times Books International, 1991).

---. "Microwave Cooking Class". *Women Without Men* (Times Books International, 2000).

Lydia Kwa. *Pulse* (Key Porter Books, 2010). Reissued (Ethos Books, 2014.)

Madeleine Lee. "five spice". *flinging the triplets* (firstfruits publications, 2015).

Margaret Louise Devadason. "Scramble". *OF ZOOS* (Issue 8.1 Dec 2018 / Jan 2019).

Margaret Leong. "Night". *Rivers to Senang* (Eastern Universities Press, 1958).

Meiko Ko. "The Satay Monologues". *A Luxury We Must Afford*. Eds. Christine Chia, Joshua Ip, and Cheryl Julia Lee (Math Paper Press 2016).

Nabilah Said. "Comfort Food". *Twenty-Four Flavours: Salted Vegetables and Duck Soup* (Math Paper Press, 2014).

Ng Yi-Sheng. "mock meat". *Last Boy* (firstfruits publications, 2006).

Ruth Tang. "Crabs to Slow Cooking". *SingPoWriMo 2016: The Anthology.* Eds. Joshua Ip, Daryl Qilin Yam and Ruth Tang (Math Paper Press, 2016).

Shirley Geok-lin Lim. "Brinjal". *Modern Secrets* (Dangaroo Press, 1989).

---. "First Addiction". *Ars Poetica for the Day* (Ethos Books, 2015).

---. "Mango". *What the Fortune Teller Didn't Say* (West End Press, 1998).

Stephanie Chan. "When the World Ends You Will Be Eating Hokkien Mee". *Roadkill for Beginners* (Math Paper Press, 2019).

Sushiro (now Omoté). "commonplace chirashi frolics...". Omoté Facebook Page (Aug 8 2018).

---. "In one's element...". Omoté Facebook Page (Jul 9 2018).

---. "sea-water sea urchin coherence...". Omoté Facebook Page (Jul 13 2018).

Theophilus Kwek. "As if they'd been waiting". *Circle Line* (Math Paper Press, 2013).

Toh Hsien Min. "Aubergines". *Means to an End* (Landmark Books, 2008).

---. "Durians". *Means to an End* (Landmark Books, 2008).

Tse Hao Guang. "Apples". *SingPoWriMo 2016: The Anthology*. Eds. Joshua Ip, Daryl Qilin Yam and Ruth Tang (Math Paper Press 2016).

Wahid Al Mamun. "Gulab Jamun". *Anima Methodi: The Poetics of Mirroring*. Eds. Desmond Kon Zhicheng-Mingdé, and Eric Tinsay Valles (Squircle Line Press, 2018).

Wong May. "The Queue". *Superstitions* (Harcourt Brace Jovanovich, 1978).

---. "Sleeping with Tomatoes". *Picasso's Tears: Poems 1978-2013* (Octopus Books, 2014).

---. "Wild Strawberries". *Superstitions* (Harcourt Brace Jovanovich, 1978).

Wong Phui Nam. "Drinking Wine – Two Poems (Li Bai)". *Against the Wilderness* (Blackwater Books, 2000).

Yong Shu Hoong. "Tanglin Halt". *The Viewing Party* (Ethos Books, 2013).